PARIS CALLING

What it Takes to Pull up Stakes

DOUG PIOTTER

Copyright © 2025 by Doug Piotter

All rights reserved.

No portion of this book may be reproduced in any form without written permission from the publisher or author, except as permitted by U.S. copyright law.

Contents

1. Message Received 2013 — 1
2. The Catalyst 2015 — 7
3. The Handler — 13
4. Most People are Nice — 24
5. Downsizing — 29
6. A Little About Us — 36
7. Bugged Out — 49
8. San Francisco Consulate — 54
9. Touch Down — 61
10. Only Sick Above the Neck — 67
11. Un Peu de Puissance — 76
12. Construction Sherpa — 82
13. Charming Mothers and Conjured Grandmas — 90
14. An Unforgettable Chapter — 96
15. In the Tube — 104
16. Epic Paris Apartment Hunt — 112
17. I Get Around — 118
18. Where Have I Been? — 129

19.	The View from Montmartre	133
20.	Balls and Noses	140
21.	Public Storage and the Dystopian Hellscape	144
22.	Banksy Hiding in Plain Sight	148
23.	French Crack and a Strong Note on Cheese	154
24.	The Big Table	160
25.	Locked Out	165
26.	Le Tour, all Over the Map	169
27.	Thalasso Fiasco	178
28.	Academy of Grift	186
29.	Paris Emptied Out and Then Some	190
30.	Fifty Shades of Gravy	199
31.	Post Script Wrap-up	209

Chapter 1
Message Received 2013

I've made choices that landed me in prison, and I've made choices that landed me in Paris. Paris is better. I can't pinpoint the exact moment my switch flipped to illuminate Paris, but I like to think the idea has always flickered in my subconscious. The fleeting thoughts I'd have about living abroad seemed far-fetched and treasonous. They danced in and out, sometimes burning bright, as part of my lifelong desire to connect with my French roots, the side of my family I never knew. I would repeatedly chalk them up to flights of fancy, snap out of it, and go about my business. But as circumstances changed, the thoughts got more aggressive. So in my mind's eye, over time, down came the red, white and blue, and up went the blue, white and red.

My wife gravitated towards European sensibilities, having lived in Italy as a girl. She had gone on and on about her desire to live in Paris for the eleven years we'd been together. I didn't know it then, but the desire would become contagious. The first time she divulged her lust for living in France, I was barely two months out of prison and rigid as an oak plank. I barfed out, "I'd rather live in Spokane." I knew nothing of Spokane, except what a friend I'd done time with had told me. You can take the man out of prison, but the prison always lingers.

She said, "You should think bigger." As is often the case, my reasoning lacked substance. She was right, I was guilty of thinking small. In prison I was self-assured, but in the real world, pangs of self-loathing crept up on me. I thought, *after all the trouble I've been responsible for, it doesn't seem right that I shouldn't still suffer.* Spokane would've fit the bill. She made clear that she didn't have to suffer—which gave me pause—then reminded me that I was my own captain, that I'd paid my dues and I got to choose. With the opportunity to latch onto the thought process of a sane and sober woman, it would be food for thought during my upcoming accelerated growth cycle.

My first treat on my first trip to Paris. Sublime!

My first trip to Paris was a birthday gift to my wife. We were riding high after I'd completed a fire restoration and received my biggest paycheck to date. The homeowner was sleeping one off when his dryer's jam-packed lint trap caught fire. The blaze whooshed up the stairwell and through the roof. His fleet-footed neighbor pulled him out, gifting him another day of life and another hangover. I had to take the roof off, strip the entire house down to bare studs and seal in the smell with a special paint. I filled four, thirty-five-yard dumpsters with a lifetime of his smoke-damaged belongings. It was a four-month work marathon and an epic battle with the insurance company's claims adjuster to get him to properly pony up. I was ready for an adventure.

I didn't have the means or inclination to travel until 2009. So, at forty-nine, for my first time out of the country, I traveled to Puerto Vallarta, Mexico, to stay at our friends' beautiful house that they built out of cement, tile and wrought iron, at the edge of the jungle above the Río Cuale River. It was Thanksgiving, and I passed on the years-long tradition of driving my mom down to my sister Vicki's house in Oregon. That year, she'd have to rough it at my sister Pam's house in a Seattle suburb with her in-laws—who she pretended she didn't like—and her lovable grandchildren. The truth is, my mom was painfully shy but came off as a bit snooty.

I generally had to pry my mom out of her apartment to make those trips, let alone to the grocery store. As a true sceptic, she said, "Why would you want to go to Mexico?" Up 'til then, we both thought our individual slices of Seattle were about all there was to the world. I am delighted to admit how wrong I'd been.

April is the perfect time for a first trip to Paris, not too crowded, with bursts of rain followed by brilliant blue skies. As soon as we were out of the Metro tunnel and on the Paris streets, Terrell became emotionally feverish. I too had become tainted with emotion. Hit with a feast for the senses, we wobbled on our lower extremities and held hands, looking goofy, at the carved stone medieval architecture on Île-Saint-Louis—one of the little islands on the Seine. Every architect put a personal stamp on their buildings. There's no such thing as cookie cutter in France. Seems there was an ongoing beauty contest when it came to construction with no obvious winners and clearly no losers.

We were confronted with whiffs of perfume, countered by hefty wafts from the sewer—a little something for everyone. I was shocked to learn that not everyone in Paris was a tourist, people really did live and work here. When we were in line and it came time to board the plane to Seattle, after our ten-day blink of an eye, Terrell sobbed—because, happy or sad, that's how she's wired. Filtered through her snot bubbles came the words: "I'm not going back."

Sure, she'd tossed out riddles like that before, so I asked, "What do you mean?"

She said, "Maybe you have to go, but I don't." It took the entire contents of my vocabulary sack to coax her on board the soon-to-abandon-us plane, back to Seattle. I shot an index finger skyward and made a valiant proclamation, "One day soon, we shall return. I promise" which was just enough to get her on the plane. The crowd queued up to board was as relieved as I was.

I didn't realize I wasn't just blowing smoke and that the stars would realign. Moving to Paris wasn't always paramount, but staying married was. Once back home, we toyed with the idea of what it would take to move to France and vowed to revisit the conversation. To my wife's delight, little by little, the idea gained traction and took on a sense of urgency. Spokane was dead to me.

Before I got sober, the trajectory of my disease had me whittle my possessions down to nothing, which made homelessness more manageable. As an odd man out, whistling in the dark, I convinced myself, *to conform to the norm is a sucker's game,* that by traveling light and by night, I was a winner. I still don't claim to be normal, but stone-cold sober, I travel by day, know who I am, and choose to sleep indoors.

Quite the contrast from when my life had been stripped down to a single, black plastic bag full of dreck, nothing more than a security blanket I'd drag from one encampment to the next. It housed the entirety of my heavy, hollow life. Then I joined prison (twice), and let those keepers go. Twelve years later—by lessons learned from bad behavior—I wormed my way out of the can, with shiny and softened edges.

One month out of prison I met my future wife. Two years later, in the summer of '04, we bought our first house together, a modest, but solid mid-century rambler in the burbs for a list price of $200,000. It had a pulldown ladder that accessed the attic crawlspace. When I climbed into the attic, I smelled what seemed like fresh cut cedar, as if the house had just been built. I knew we had stumbled upon a gem.

At the time, mortgage brokers were like magicians, and banks offered no-down-payment mortgages. Good thing, because we were both stone cold broke. The cherubic faced baller who levitated us asked my wife, "How much do you make as an artist?"

The answer was, "not much." I noticed the lineup of DIY trophies crowding her office shelf for being, *Broker of the Year, ...the Century*, and beyond, as well as some religious tchotchkes. She looked at me, "And you?" Same answer.

Seems she couldn't work with that few zeroes, so she violently shook her pen and said, "I'm just going put down $100,000." And with a master stroke, she inked our fate. We signed and walked out with a house, for a song and dance. I later learned she may have embellished, while gathering all those accolades. It was an open door to the middle class. I'm forever grateful I stepped over the threshold.

We had arrived, caught up in a cyclone to accumulate. We soon ran out of space, sold that one and bought a roomier, second house, which we quickly maxed out with belongings—a step up from stuff. Then, Terrell and I sold the second house to buy a bigger, third house, and filled that too—the American dream, rinse and repeat. *I sometimes wonder if Rumi lived in a big house.*

After our trip to Paris, serendipity gifted us a copy of Marie Kondo's book, *The Life-Changing Magic of Tidying Up*. We had nowhere to put it, but accepted it anyway, because we were curious to see what all the buzz was about a skinny little book, no more than a pamphlet, that happened to sell millions of copies. We spent the next two years in subconscious preparation, by pairing down our belongings.

Chapter 2
The Catalyst 2015

Pre-prison, I didn't win any Citizen of the Year awards. Although the Post Office *did* think enough of me to put up the cover of *Doin' Time* magazine and say a few words. Believe me, I wasn't somebody you would've wanted living in *your* bushes. Nor was I a candidate for neighborhood Block Watch Captain.

The rights and duties of citizenship never really spoke to me until I was able to cast my first vote, for forty-four, at forty-eight. Yes, we can!

Before that, I didn't much care who sat behind the desk—made from the oak timbers of the 18th century British ship HMS Resolute—in the Oval Office, or who was on my City's Council, or what was on their agenda. Unless funding my habit was to come up for vote. I had to get mine the old-fashioned way, theft. I worked overtime with my pet project of reducing the scourge of street drugs, as a humanitarian effort, so you didn't have to. You're welcome. Of course, this was long before GoFundMe existed.

All of that changed after I completed my sentence for multiple bank robberies, which included the fourteen years it took me to pay back the money. I had plenty of time to ponder the emotional harm I'd caused all those bank tellers. As part of my amends, I wrote them letters—which my lawyer delivered—acknowledging the fact that I'd robbed them of their peace of mind, with a promise to do better in the future.

*To keep the trees from taking over our lake view,
I'd climb up thirty feet, tree to tree, with an
array of tools. It was truly a labor of love..*

After I cleaned up, I got out and talked a woman into marrying me, started a business, accepted a two hundred-thousand-dollar bank loan for a house, capitulated to the taxman, mowed the lawn, and cleaned out the—sweet smell of success—cat box. I was happy to do all of it, as I made the most of my second chance. Although at times I feel like a fraud and in way over my head, like I'm living someone else's life. But I really have come to enjoy being the town square. I tell you this because considering where I came from, the odds that I beat were truly long.

Just when I started to carry my own weight and get in the groove of blending in with the rest of humanity who grind it out, the universe took a dump. Enter Agent Orange, who for some ungodly reason, still hangs in the air and challenges my love for country. I felt a little short changed.

There are things I wish I'd have done before I bugged out. I've never seen the Grand Canyon or Niagara Falls, a Vermont autumn, or skied the Rockies. Never been to a Broadway show, a jazz club in Harlem or seen what, in New Mexico, had inspired Georgia O'Keefe's vagina flowers. My curiosity still thirsts.

Pain is mandatory, but suffering is optional. I've kicked this pragmatic complexity around the block for over thirty-one years. After returning from our first visit to France in 2013, I was so enamored by what I saw, that to my wife's delight, I posed the question, "What would it take to live in Paris?" Then I looked around and wondered, *Who said that?*

We started to entertain the related questions leaked by my internal adventurer. They nibbled and gnawed, before ripping chunks. We made pro and con lists, ad nauseam. We put it on the back burner and bided our time. Then came Trump, the accelerant that sped things along. That was the moment the voice inside my head got belligerent and poked at me that it was time for us to move our feet. Intuition has served me well. In prison, it saved me from a host of trick bags. So, when someone repeatedly shows me who they are, I tend to believe them.

Another thought that had been bludgeoning my psyche was this: *There are many ways to live a life. I'm not getting any younger, so, if not now, when?*

Even though my father was a prick and liked to think of himself as a supreme ruler, he did take time out from barking long distance commands at us to fight fascism in WWII. That's something I can admire. One thing to love about France is all the visual reminders—plaques on schools, war memorials, etc.—that explain why Nazis should fuck the fuck off.

My wife is Jewish, so to see U.S. politicians goose step on eggshells around the issue of white nationalism while celebrating a grifter, disturbed the living hell out of us. Human failings drive me to distraction. Absurdism and satire, during the rise of global fascism has helped keep me snark-raving sane and say yes to my pent-up aspirations. I draw a breath.

Most people go the direction they are headed. So, when the Nazis infiltrated Washington D.C., my wife and I voted with our feet and boarded a plane to France. Born of hard experience, she'd been taught by her grandmother what to look for. And we were seeing it.

A Momentary Pause.

As I sit here in real time, looking out the seventh-floor window of my Montmartre apartment, sipping harsh, half-roasted coffee—because French roast doesn't exist in France—I look out in awe at the beauty of the Paris rooftops which lead to *La Basilique du Sacré-Coeur de Montmartre*. Seven years living in Paris, and I'm still on pink cloud number nine. It remains surreal and has yet to disappoint.

I spin the clock back to 2016, a time before the start of the Zombie Apocalypse. It seems like a thousand Stephen King novels ago. My small-scale construction business in Seattle was going gangbusters. Sixteen years as a business owner was fully starting to pay off. I'd just published a book and was constructing more suspect sentences in preparation for another. I felt I was on my way. I just didn't know that after I awoke from my election-induced coma, it would be to the French Consulate in San Francisco requesting permission to enter France.

After shaming all his contenders out of existence, the NRC's chosen one emerged. The orange toxin blew onto every TV screen in the Western world. Ha ha ha ha ha. I couldn't stop laughing. I thought, *This is your guy?* a guy who fit Gandhi's description of the seven deadly sins: Wealth without work, pleasure without conscience, science without humanity, knowledge without character, politics without principle, commerce without morality and worship without sacrifice. Not to mention wife without documentation.

When asked about the criminal amount of free campaign airtime he gifted the human gag reflex, Jeffrey Zucker, CNN's CEO said, "Good for CNN, bad for America." Duh! The usurper rode down the escalator with infectious disease Stephen Miller, and his scorched earth policies tucked under his arm. Together, they would start the process of defoliation.

Through the course of the election process, the collective mood of Seattle's shrinking left had gone from sick fascination to election night Kubler Ross—minus the acceptance—to deep, dark depression. The morning after, I woke up monosyllabic. *WTF?* The Dunning-Kruger effect had prevailed. In my mind, the Statue of Liberty's value had dropped to $1.55 per pound.

I looked out the window and drooled. I fled to the island nation of Catatonia. My limited creative juices turned to dust and blew away. I didn't care about books or building kitchens. And, I didn't write or read anything, except for bad news, over and over, for almost five months. I became obsessed with unearthing a smoking-gun that would set things right. I was like a crackhead on a deep carpet safari. It was a staggering time-suck, time I will never get back. I was, at that point, radically alone. My wife, with whom I lived, was also alone, because, *Sorry Doug's not home right now, he's busy sparring with loonies on social media.* I'd become unavailable.

A light started to flicker. Terrell and I landed on the idea of being alone together, *Over there.* Starting anew began to tantalize and pop the corn that fed our consciousness. *Over there,* people enjoy life and are kind to each other. *Over there,* Liberté, Fraternité, and Égalité matter. *Over there,* regardless of affiliation, the government seems to like more than forty percent of its people.

"I like pastries, why not," I said. It was on.

Next came the long, late-night discussions about the seriousness of our outrageous inclination. Things yet to be done, how it could all play out, and major adjustments to be made if we were to make the leap. We could never have figured things out on our own brainpower. Against my natural inclination, I heeded my wife's advice to enlist help. Our neighbors Sam and Suzanne, during countless rap sessions, helped steer us towards what mattered most. And a host of others fed us delicate slices of wisdom. Was this thing that we both longed for illusory, or would we be shoo-ins?

Soon, our collective desire ached to be satisfied. We started to smell baguettes and see ourselves as French. We made vision boards, to help us manifest and pinned them to the wall. Fields of lavender exploded around us. In my head, I was bona fide French—I've got the crooked teeth to prove it. Itchy feet and forward motion would take us around the bend.

Dining room of our last Seattle house, set for a dinner party.

Chapter 3
The Handler

A Vision Without a Plan is a Hallucination. In 2016 my wife stumbled upon a serendipitous event, a presentation at the Franco-American Society about the merits of immigrating to France. On her way out the door, I said, "Hey, bring me back a couple cans of SpaghettiOs, will ya?"

The woman presenting had fled the Pacific Northwest some years earlier, but occasionally snuck back in to give a talk, and sell her freshly plucked, Pyrénées goose down contraband comforters. I was intrigued and couldn't wait to be spoon-fed the details.

After her talk, she told my wife we should go see a French woman who went the other direction and escaped the evils of socialism in favor of unfettered capitalism. She lived near the Microsoft campus, one of the capitalism capitals of the world, and specialized in the punishing stateside administrative tasks necessary for such an epic move. The expat who gave the talk said she couldn't have made the move to France without this insider knowledge. Even though the woman of whom she spoke exited the U.S. years before, when the mood was very different, our interest—mine, through gradual, unconscious assimilation, my wife's, predetermined and set in stone—was piqued. So, we scratched up some capital and hired her for a couple of consultations.

It was evident at the onset that our consultant had a buttoned-up point of view. She offered her heartfelt negative opinions based on status quo. We politely listened, uninspired. We knew we were going for it with or without her blessing. And we were willing to fail. We felt the political ground rapidly crater under our feet and focused on conjuring up the spirit of a softer, gentler Generation X consulate staff who would see into our hearts, rubber stamp our stacks of paperwork, and lobby on our behalf to the French Government. So, we took what we liked from the consultant and left the rest. Call it intuition, or what you will, but in 2018, a year after Macron took office, the Consulate gatekeeper's requirements did soften up a bit.

In France, the population doesn't consider dumbfuckery a badge of honor. Intellectuals are held in high regard, equal to sports or rock stars in the U.S. I knew my wife would qualify and thought I might slip through the cracks if I could keep my mouth shut. Our handler felt very strongly that we keep our house, but the *For Sale* sign was already cemented in our heads and we needed the cash to qualify. She also told us we'd need to move to a village first, then over time, work our way into one of the big cities where life happens. That notion conjured pangs.

I knew nothing about villages, or even The Villages people in Florida. But villages are villages, and—no offense to villages—I had no intention of being just another village idiot. I wanted to be a city idiot. There's no denying that I'm a city boy. It's where the action is. When a friend asked if I wanted to go camping, I said, "You mean outside, on the ground, in a tent? That's called homelessness, been there, done that. I'll get a hotel instead." My wife feels the same way. She says, when Hermès starts making camping tents, she'll reconsider. Not that we'd have to live in a tent, but, c'mon man, *a village?* So, with Paris being the center of the universe, we respectfully pooh-poohed that slice of advice.

I teased, "I'm a writer," to the consultant, knowing the jury was still out, but hoping it would be weighty. It was an idiotic proclamation that had no bearing. A way for me to hug myself without wearing a straitjacket.

She asked, "What is it that you write about?"

I detailed my bottom shelf, laugh-riot memoir about the horrors of drug addiction, bank robbery, my decade in prison and the joys of recovery. Her flat-lined expression told me she wouldn't be my ideal reader and the French government wouldn't be either. She warned, "Don't volunteer information that could preclude you from qualifying," suggesting I keep my life's gnarly nuggets to myself. If I really wanted to Frenchify, I still had the right to remain silent. Prudent advice which I *did* take to heart. It hadn't occurred to me that I still might be considered an unstable atomic nucleus with the potential for radioactive decay. Even though I would eventually pass muster at the consulate, I anguished 'til the plane landed and I'd made it through customs, un-accosted.

My wife, with a successful thirty-year art career, was laser focused on the *Passport Talent* visa for artists, but was told, "You need to be famous to receive an artist's visa. *Pour vous, ce n'est pas possible.*" Bummer, Debbie Downer.

Terrell ended up applying for a work visa but sent images of her artwork anyway. My focus was a little murky, as I had yet to solidify what I wanted to be when I grew up. I do a lot of bragging about my wife and for good reason. She hadn't spoken French in thirty years when she started her studies anew. She decided that she could handle the paperwork aspect. On that front, all I could offer was moral support. She may as well have brought along a mushroom for morel support, because at the time, I was an electrified container of uncertainty. We appreciated that risk would be part of the adventure. We needed to believe, and all the doom and gloom didn't set well with either of us. That's when we decided to cut our handler loose.

Due to the consulate website crashing and catching fire after the stampede caused by the 2016 election upheaval, it took multiple attempts to log in, but we were finally able to break through the firewall and confirm an appointment. We had no plan B.

There was another piece of advice from our handler which we *did* value. She told me to think twice about signing up to start a business before I got there. The French are famous for paperwork and the stack required would be fat. The fine print indicated that I would need workspace, machinery, employees, insurance for all, a fire inspection and—death to the notion—language skills. *Je suis désolé, je n'en ai pas.* She bid us adieu as our thoughts leaned towards San Francisco for an appointment with the French Consulate, our new higher power. I shuttered my construction company after sixteen years and figured I could always jump back in once in Paris. I had no idea how pie in the sky that thought was. Miraculously, my pie would be on the ground and accessible once I landed.

FIRST HOUSE LISTING, APRIL 2017

All in, we listed our stunning, ten-year, lakeview labor of love on the red-hot Seattle real estate market. Flush techies had converged on Seattle to bid each other into submission. They lunged at and gobbled up anything with four walls, forcing prices up and Seattleites out. So, based on obscene wealth and frenzied buying jags, we were convinced we would strut into Europe swinging our big bag of USDs. Then reality bit. We pulled our listing after nary an offer. Once our disappointment subsided, we parked our plan for a spell, to face our disturbing American reality.

The 2,450 square foot Seattle property we let go of to be in 500 square feet in Paris.

After leaking our French wanderlust to a new friend, she raised an eyebrow, casually blew on her freshly painted fingernails and said, "I own a house in France."

I raised my own eyebrow and thought, *sure you do.* "Tell me more."

She said, "It's south, in Riolas." She went on to explain that her husband had been an engineering guru at Airbus airplane manufacturer in Toulouse but committed treason to work for Boeing in Seattle. At the time, Boeing's planes were just six months away from falling out of the sky and being deemed space junk.

"If you want," she said, "you guys can stay there, no one else is. Just pay the caretaker five hundred euros for utilities for the three weeks you'll be there. He lives in an outbuilding, you won't be bothered." After a month of public real estate shaming, we were ready to treat ourselves to a little getaway. First Riolas and Barcelona, then the center of the universe, Paris. I thought, *five weeks in Europe was sure to absorb some of the sting*. So, we set our desires in motion and booked a flight to French Mayberry.

This is when we embarked on our second visit, but first reconnaissance to France, hell-bent on relocation. We hadn't sold, but that didn't stop us from pinching a little equity—a salve to sooth our wounded souls.

Our first Paris vacation, four years prior, hijacked our sensibilities and—three days lost to the flu aside—opened our eyes to a world full of history, wonder and SOS Médecins, the doctors who make housecalls on bicycles for seventy euros. On our second trip, becoming Parisian took over like a brain eating virus.

The Riolas house reminded me of a cobbled together house I looked at during the Seattle housing boom of the mid 2000s, when faux contractors popped up like poisonous mushrooms. Because, with the simplicity of electrical, heating, plumbing, structural systems and aesthetics, what could be so hard about properly remodeling a house? Mr. Faux-it had removed just about every load-bearing wall from the house of Jenga and used the lumber to build himself a special lookout tower of despair. He noticed me puzzling over the exposed wiring and scabbed together drywall scraps.

He beamed, "I did it *all* myself."

I said, "Impressive." It resembled a tweaker's crime-scene, like the house in my hood where the dad, dressed in a suit, would go off to work with briefcase in hand and by the time he got home, his son would have scrapped a few more pieces of the aluminum siding until the house was down to bare plywood.

Our agent got on her agents-only website and said, "You no longer own this house, it's gone into foreclosure." She asked, who's *so-and-so*? The name on the deed was his soon-to-be ex-wife. His face morphed.

The house in Riolas, though not quite as egregious, *did* sit outside of reality as related to floor plans or building codes. It had been purchased sight unseen, an "affordable" house with a haphazard layout. Riolas didn't look to be beholden to any pesky rules and regulations regarding building standards. The dwelling was nothing more than a single-story cinder block starfish. Arms reached out in all directions from the main hub. The dark hallways cloaked bedrooms with jail cell-sized windows and baths behind uninviting doors.

When the adventuresome couple ditched out for America, they were left with the exercise of trying to sell a poorly insulated, architecturally challenged structure they didn't want and no longer needed, on land required by French law to produce food. So, cold and lonely, there the house sat, in the middle of a stunning farmland tapestry with the snow-capped Pyrénées as a backdrop. Out of doors was the place to be.

Riolas is centered in the Haute-Garonne region of Midi-Pyrénées, smack dab between the Atlantic Ocean and Mediterranean Sea, close to the Spanish border. To smooth the way for our adventure, I bought Peter Mayle's blockbuster book: *A Year in Provence,* a book about turning around a distressed French property—which is still on my list of to-dos. The jacket bragged, "Over six million copies sold." *Probably, a buddy of Marie Kondo.* Sick with envy, I made it six-million and one and loved it all the way to France, on a Boeing, praying we'd maintain altitude.

At the car rental agency, I hotdogged my Luddite status to the agent, "We don't need GPS, we'll make do with a *real* map." My wife shot me a, *who's we?* look. Blinded by frugality, I snapped it open for emphasis, ripping it down the middle.

The agent said, "You will not find Riolas on any map." He clasped his hands, "I implore you to make use of the GPS. It's simple." I too, was simple. He was so freaked out that this American idiot and his—had it up to here—wife would get lost in the French countryside, full of skinny, savage boar, that he slashed the additional cost in half and half again.

I soon learned that there's no such thing as 'as the crow flies,' in rural France, unless the crow is drunk. I worked that GPS relentlessly; it was worth every penny. The roads wound 'round and 'round the Rorschach shaped plots of farmland. One missed turn could have put us in Spain. I began to wonder if Riolas existed at all. But it *did* exist, and it turned out to be a great base camp for exploring the south of France.

The day we arrived, the French Presidential primaries were in full swing. The process was nothing like the bloated and wasteful dark money slugfest we'd just been bludgeoned with in the divided States. In the French election, each candidate receives a measly eight million euros to do with as they wish. They could have parked it where the sun don't shine—on the backside of a sunflower—if they'd wanted to.

Emmanuel Macron rose above the crowded field of moderates angling for top dog status in France's top doghouse, the Élysée Palace, to face far-right nut job Marine Le Pen, in the election's second round, two weeks later. After a public endorsement from the nine disposed moderates, who collectively said, *France can't afford to cannibalize itself by electing a White Nationalist* in the general election, Macron beat Marine Le Pen two to one. The country became more inviting, and *Monsieur le Président* opened the doors to some of the mass exodus of talent that bolted from the U.S. at the start of Trump's dumbing down, anti-education, pro-dipshit campaign. France welcomed educators, innovators, artists, scientists, musicians, etc., anyone who could contribute to the betterment of the country. Visualize no election fatigue. We thought, *why not us?*

The Riolas property's caretaker was a Brit so broke, he'd been reusing teabags. He couldn't believe his good fortune being transported to the land of milk, honey, and fresh teabags, via a 500 € utilities fund. He scooped up the cash and promptly dematerialized.

Upon arrival, the first thing we did was don rubber gloves, disinfect the unused bleach bottle, then use the contents to disinfect what would be our three-week nest. Because the house was elevated, the deck provided a

Grandma Moses style panoramic view of the farmhouses, until the dots disappeared into the breadth of the mountains.

Despite the April sunshine, and the replenished utility fund, the house stayed stone cold. Even if the utilities got paid—which they didn't—cinder block houses are notoriously hard to heat. The wool had been pulled over our eyes, which, I guess, is better than nothing. I thought *an ember must flicker, somewhere, if I could just get to the end of a hall and through the winning door.* Lack of heat had never been so expensive.

On occasion, the don't caretaker would duck in to smudge up the kitchen cabinets with his signature jam prints. I learned to appreciate the heat produced by the prickly quill wounds of the featherbed.

No matter the size, every village has a grand cathedral as its cornerstone, with World War One memorials on display to commemorate the local boys lost in *la Grande Guerre*. Impending death to democracy wasn't the only thing that drove our desire to relocate, France has plenty to offer and the French are trusting. While visiting one such cathedral, priceless artifacts hung low like grapes. There was a sign which read: *Please don't touch the art, or we'll be compelled to call the mayor.* There is so much impressive art in the villages, one Loire Valley church didn't know they possessed a 1510 Sandro Botticelli painting until recently. They thought it must have been a replica. They had it restored and hung it higher up on the wall as a precaution. In my Seattle neighborhood, I couldn't even trust that the plastic Frosty lawn decoration wouldn't be stolen on Christmas and set up in a front yard two doors down.

The buzz suggested the one-and-only restaurant in the village was very good, but its fickle Chef rarely unlatched the doors. If there was a code to crack, no one in the village seemed to know what it was. We cornered him one agreeable day and managed to plead our case for a seat at the table. We weren't disappointed. He served up a divine southern French meal, a whopping platter of *magret de canard* (duck breast) and a molten cabbage casserole swimming in Gruyère, which produced quite the afterlife. I couldn't wait to go back, but the doors remained latched. I'm forced to stay satisfied on my seared memory.

I later encountered a trusting, but naive, escapee from a nearby farm, where ducks are raised for France's canard crazy consumers. He'd found his way to the jam-packed outdoor market for a last look around before the paddy wagon hauled him back to the farm for decapitation. He was such a behemoth that we near looked eye to eye. Dead duck walking—as handsome a beast ever to waddle death row, continues to live in my dreams.

Out exploring, we discovered that Toulouse is a nice day trip, if you can navigate the endless roundabouts that threaten to shoot you off into one of the many farmer's fields. The landlocked, big-money private microstate of Andorra—not to be confused with a fluffy bunny—is in proximity. It's a great place to visit, if you're rolling in it, so I'm told. If it's commercial you crave, there's also Carcassonne, a sort of Gothic-Romanesque Disney Land. Highly popular with the knee-high sock wearing, summer ski pole swinging crowd on the hunt for medieval knick-knackery. If your navigation does break down, at dusk the sunflowers point west, until you reach the sea.

Terrell appropriated a Riolas neighbor's dog for a walk.

Chapter 4
Most People are Nice

Out for a Sunday drive, we found ourselves lost and running on fumes in the French countryside at twilight. Resident genius had bypassed a handful of stations. "We're good, we're good," then coasting into station number six, "not good" and it was too late. Over time, my penchant for digging up trouble has quit producing spectacular jail-time upheavals, but I can still be annoying, perhaps criminally so, to my wife. After I stepped in it, blissed turned to pissed.

I smiled weakly into her baleful eyes, and said, "I've been thinking in gallons. It's the only way to accurately measure what kind of mileage these babies get." That's how I rolled, to a dead stop, at the last petrol station on an oh-so lonely French highway outside Toulouse. I was beyond sorry. I was beyond the pale. My wife burned hot. Watching the topped off cars whiz by, she said, "Funny, nobody else seems to be running out of gas." I searched my mental index for a riotous rebuttal but thought better of it.

Then came the sound of crickets. The last pump before marriage counseling didn't take cash, and wouldn't accept our suspect American bankcards, so we hunkered down in the looming darkness to accept our fate as Sunday night panhandlers. I *did* have extensive experience with that, so I nudged my French speaking wife out the car to prospect.

In a moment of inspiration, she flagged down a bicycle and said, *"J'ai un grand problème!"* My underdeveloped acumen questioned, *Bicycle? How're we supposed to siphon gas from a bicycle?* The peculiar rider was a wiry

Fashion Week Jesus. *"Dites-moi,"* he said. She provided a short, tear-filled, but not hysterical, burst of details. I provided self-pity, which is *not* nothin'. He stroked his Freudian beard, dug into his eight hundred euro blazer pocket and produced his bank card, which opened the petrol tap and a small window into a happy marriage. Whoop, whoop, free gas y'all! Usually something I supply.

When we offered cash and genuflections, our benefactor waived us off. *"C'est normal,"* he said, trusting we'd stop the pump at the twenty euro mark. He then rode off towards the disappearing fireball in search of additional marriages on the brink.

RISKS ABOUND

It took a lot of reassurance and preparation to put our house in order and walk away from a comfortable middle-class mirage that didn't quite seem to fit either of us. Ultimately, it would be up to us to wake up and snap ourselves out of American dream for an honorable discharge. Luckily, we were both called to do so. Neither of us had ever been averse to taking risks. They haven't always panned out or been prudent, but the tightrope has always remained under my feet.

Here are a few of the risks I've taken over the years, in no specific order. I worked for a drunken sea captain who steered into the fog with holes in his net. I married a Jehovah's Witnesses and with a crazed, but docile gang, knocked on doors on Saturdays, only to have crapped out before Jacob could drop me his ladder. Fast and furious, I injected speedballs with paranoid, gun-toting gangsters, convinced I'd been stealing from them (they weren't wrong) then, after the experiment worked so well, did it again. I ate at Beth's Café and if you're a true Seattleite, you know how dangerous that could be. I hit on a psych nurse and was *still* only on the locked ward making wallets for five days. I robbed banks, volunteered for prison and shaved my head without joining a prison gang. I got sober, became vulnerable, walked with my wife—med free—through menopause and exposed my awful truths. And the beat goes on. My wife has taken plenty of risks too. She set up camp with me and led the way to France. So far, I think it has worked out swell.

I CAN BE GRATEFUL, A BRIEF RECOLLECTION

In my old hood, two gang bangers shot each other dead, landing face down in their refried beans. One minute breaking tortillas, the next, homicide statistics. The scorecard in *The Stranger,* Seattle's alternative newspaper read, "Humanity two, scumbags zero." The staff at Maya's Mexican restaurant, on Rainier Avenue South, didn't sweat the bullets and the doors were closed no longer than it took to clean up the mess. Patrons queued up, the table was cleared, margaritas were poured and dinner was served. Business as usual—dinner theater, with an edge. Life goes on in Glock-heavy South Seattle, until it doesn't.

There was so much shoot-em-up in the south end of Seattle that it became part of the soundtrack to my suburban life. Like the sound of the jackhammer in Paris, one gets used to it, or dies trying. I've not heard one single muzzle blast since I moved to France.

SECOND HOUSE LISTING, AUGUST 2017

The second time the real estate sign got stuck in the dirt, there was no turning back. We vacillated between inviting the idea of failure and disapproval back in the mix, or blind trust that this time, just the right person would appear to help fund our manic wanderlust. With August being a hotter month for real estate than March, we leaned towards not growing old in the burbs and again pulled the trigger to list. Our house sold in six days to one of Bezos's Blue Origin rocket scientists who'd considered buying it in March and pondered until August. He paid just over asking price.

Terrell's handmade, hand-painted tiles in process of installation.

He got the nouveau custom built—by me—shaker-style kitchen cabinets and the hand painted tiled backsplash, with one hundred sixty-seven of my wife's individual glazed terracotta paintings. He got the custom wall colors, Terrell's handmade silk curtains, the uptown millwork, the antique chandelier, the white quartz rockery I'd built, stone by stone—repeatedly—until, according to my wife, it was aesthetically acceptable, the lavender-heavy, bird and bee-friendly garden, the multi-generational racoon family that lived in the cedar trees, the cedar deck, the mondo grill, the lake and mountain view and our eclectic neighbor, who always wore his nagging-wife-cancelling earmuffs.

The buyer got the France that my wife and I had recreated for ourselves in the middle of Upper Rainier Beach, in the southernmost outskirts of

Seattle. Smart guy, that rocket scientist. We had a month to shrink our belongings, put what was left in storage and vacate. The rest, like where were we going to live, we were forced to figure out the on the fly.

Terrell's stunning, multi-colored, tin-glazed terra-cotta hand-painted tiles.

Chapter 5

Downsizing

Looking back, it's amazing how many question marks hid out in our twenty-four hundred square foot domicile. How many eighteen volt battery-powered drill sets, or crystal vases does a person need to feel complete?

Many of the items in our house were like squatters. I had no idea where they came from, or how long they'd been there. Unidentified boxes elbowed each other for space under the stairs, to the ceiling in the garage and in every other nook and cranny. They begged us to look away. I'm disheartened to find out that after having kids, Marie Kondo has admittedly become somewhat of a slob. *If those kids don't bring you joy, or you haven't looked at them in six months, Marie, get rid of them.* But she did speak to me with her question, "Does it spark joy?" *Does what spark joy?* I discovered that what I'd put so much time and energy into sparked depression, enraging my inner chump. So, *GTFO*. With dogged determination, the Great Seattle Slough Off went full tilt.

We finally had things whittled down to a manageable size—so we thought—as we started floating towards France. When our flight date crept up on us, our approach morphed into frantic mode. We started flinging big, herkin' things—like tables and chairs, band saws and lawn equipment at our neighbors, at the Seattle Public school system to help fund the student's dreams and aspirations, at the local Somali community, or anyone else whose eyes lit up at the prospect of serviceable freebies. What we didn't give away, we offered at ten cents on the dollar for the purpose of expediency and two-way dignity. Putting a queen size natural latex mattress on a car's roof rack is like hoisting a hundred fifty pounds of Jell-O.

If it didn't fit in a suitcase, it wasn't coming with us.

When it was all said and done, we still had to rent two storage units. We made two subsequent trips back to Seattle for additional purges and crammed things into one, ten square foot unit, which—because of the Public Storage's rent increase binges—almost five years later, had become as expensive as the original two. What I speak of are luxury problems, in areas where areas didn't used to exist. Life in Seattle dictates that many a renter live in those units during the day.

Other than art, I couldn't say what was in storage. Most of what took us fifteen years to accumulate as a couple was gone in a couple weeks. I have no regrets. For me, letting go is a similar feeling to that of getting out of prison. For a free man with his head screwed on semi-straight and a few bucks in his pocket, the possibilities seem endless. On this flip side of life, what I now collect are experiences, relationships and memories, and if I don't lose my mental storage unit, there'll be plenty of room for all of that.

In Seattle, my house bordered the southern edge of the city. One of the most diverse zip codes in the country. A friend asked us if we would be willing to host a World Hajib Day party—a chance to get to know some of our female Muslim neighbors. Traditionally women only, but since it was my house, I was allowed to attend. Thanks ladies.

Women from all backgrounds packed in, talking world events, culture and demonstrating the proper way to wear a hajib. I was the only guy, but out of respect, agreed to wear a head covering. I was wrapped in the manner of a Saudi prince. It was the first time I'd eaten Ethiopian food. It was delicious. I had a blast.

My wife and I took a shine to a woman who, at age sixteen, escaped the unimaginable horrors of war in Somalia in the '90s. After her years-long journey, which included learning English and earning multiple degrees, she landed in Tukwila, Washington. Tukwila is where the Somali Center is. It's also home to Costco where, when she was pumping gas, an old white guy wearing a red hat spit in her face and told her to go back to where she came from. Trump had just usurped and was whipping his lizard-brain base into a lather. Just an extraordinary woman, interested in her children's and community's welfare, and only threatening to a certain ilk. Hearing about the incident infuriated me. This would become her new normal.

Ronald Reagan—neither my favorite president nor my least—said in a 1981, speech, "Our nation is a nation of immigrants. More than any other country, our strength comes from our own immigrant heritage and our capacity to welcome those from other lands. No free and prosperous nation can by itself accommodate all those who seek a better life or flee persecution. We must share this responsibility with other countries." Maybe the most intelligent thing he ever said. I'm glad that for the most part, France judges by one's actions, not by paranoia.

But systemic racism does exist in France—even in Paris. An African American woman, with children in tow, who stood in front of my wife and me while we waited to renew our visas, was given the old heave-ho by a Caucasian bureaucratic desk jockey. Not a good look. We stepped up and braced ourselves for the same treatment, but were greeted with a smile which said, *Welcome, trustworthy, white couple of European heritage,* and some helpful information. Wait, what? What happened to *Égalité*? Not always. I may have been outraged, but on that day, I dared not open my trap and tamped down the self-sabotage by zipping it.

FOR THE LOVE OF DOG

When I was twenty-three, I gave away my beloved dog, Tork. At the time, I couldn't even take care of myself. As a living amends for my forty-eighth birthday, I decided to rescue a death row dog from the Seattle animal shelter. I wanted to be the best human a dog ever had. I binge scrolled kennels on the internet, then visited the shelter a few times before I made my choice. When I walked the cell block, they'd wag, bark and nose the chain-link fence. "Choose me, choose me." But I noticed one who neither wagged nor barked, he just looked away. I caught a glimpse of his his grief-stricken eyes which affected me deeply.

I asked the attendant, "What's wrong with this guy?"

He said, "This one might be a challenge. He's lived through plenty of trauma."

I said, "Me too," and took home the most severely anti-social dog from the Seattle animal shelter—like my wife did for me after *I'd* been in the pound. I later found out that the person who abandoned him dropped him off with another dog, so abused that he didn't make it. We renamed our new family member Zinc, the ten percent which turns copper into bronze.

When we got home, my wife took him for a walk and he literally dragged her on the sidewalk while giving chase to another dog. A neighbor witnessed and said, "That's impressive." Instantly remorseful, Zinc knew he'd fucked up. We worked with him until he was as docile as a stuffed teddy bear. So much for a ferocious guard dog. His tightly wound tail unfurled and he stopped howling at sirens as he got comfortable. He didn't walk; he moseyed. And, he didn't swim, or fetch a stupid stick either. At the dog park he always stood just inside the fence, looking out. I know he was a deep thinker and on his own plane—a loner through and through—but he did love me.

Having landed in the lap of luxury, Zinc had it made. We fed him organic lamb and sweet potatoes, but he was finnicky. He'd often send meals back to the kitchen to be topped off with cheese and bacon and sometimes even that wasn't enough to get him to eat. He was also insecure and a bit paranoid. When relaxing on his personal goose down comforter, with bed-size pillow and hand made pillow case, he'd whip his head around as if someone was sneaking up on him. After he deemed things safe, he'd retreat to the comfort of licking his personal lollipop.

On beauty parlor day, my wife would don her painters mask and goggles, break out the Dremel tool and give Zinc a pedicure on the deck. This, she took on after one too many botched and bloody clippings courtesy of a veterinarian assistant's shaky hands. Once situated and comfortable, after a few rotations of the grinding wheel, I would hear a stern warning, "Knock it off." Zinc would sigh heavily, get up, reposition himself six inches out of reach, then plop himself back down. "Knock it off," Terrell said. This dance would go on in six-inch increments all the way across the deck.

Our beloved Zinc. A former death row dog turned cuddly seeker of treats. Happy to be alive after his cancerous spleen was removed.

I'm a periodical whack drummer who's been known to woodshed, an old-school musician's term for practicing alone in the basement. Woodshedding is a bit like masturbating, in that no one else will ever get anything out of it, especially not Zinc. There was a time I was so distraught over my timing that I considered throwing myself behind a train. I joke, but when I was in the throes as Bonham reincarnate, Zinc had a psychotic relapse, got loose, and attacked a German Shepherd service animal attached to a frowny-faced person.

Bad scene, man.

A dog's hearing is three times more sensitive than a humans so there's a good chance my playing, specifically the ringing of the cymbals, was doing Zinc real damage. As much as I loved my vintage '70s Rogers blue sparkle drum kit, which I bought and disassembled out from under a country band to a cacophony of boos while they played their farewell song in a smokey roadside dive bar, I loved Zinc more and set my aging rock star aspirations free. For the love of dog, I had no hesitation. It begs the question who rescued whom.

Zinc got cancer in 2015. Terrell and I moved forward with surgery to remove his spleen, which he apparently could've lived without. The surgery was successful, but his kidneys failed shortly after and he died on the winter solstice of 2015. I buried him in my back yard—which I knew was illegal—and planted a crabapple tree on top of him. It's the only law I've willfully broken since my release from prison in 2002. Zinc's death was another reason our house seemed too big and gave us permission to let it all go. Ever since, I've continued trying to be the person Zinc thought I was.

Fast forward last summer. I was lamenting to a fellow drummer about not having played for over a decade and having nowhere to set up a kit. He clued me in on *HF Music Studio,* not far from my Paris apartment. This soundproof studio is perfect for the aging rocker like me who's aiming to recapture past glory. I toil and toil, four times a week, inching ever closer to the imaginary mountain top—raaaah! It keeps me dreaming and keeps me fit. I kick it around with a new acquaintance, Kenny G.—last name not included for the purpose of anonymity—who also makes use of the space. Even though he's sold over seventy million albums, he too practices. He has no entourage and sports no visible bling—just a regular guy under the radar in Paris. We're both Seattleites with South End connections, which makes for good small talk. I was pleased to discover he's a good natured, approachable guy with a reasonable world view. The antithesis of Kanye West. In a world full of KWs, aspire to be a KG.

Chapter 6
A Little About Us

My favorite T-shirt from yesteryear read: *It's a Great Day to go sailing—if you're a dick,* a window into my upbringing. My family wore our poverty on our dirty sleeves, until we got a second-hand washing machine. Neither me, nor my wife have ever been in the yacht club or sported a pair of Sperry Topsiders. White trash Yahtzee parties were about as highfalutin as it got for me as a kid.

"The Path of Repentance." Signage on a steep road in Aix-en-Provence.

I no longer have it out for those who are monied and I do have friends who suffer the internal strife of being trust funded, though I am thankful they don't flap their jibs too much about it. All I inherited was a damaged psyche, a bowling ball and a hard head. I came up with the reckless abandon all on my own.

My wife was born with talent, intelligence and an unshakeable vision of one day moving to Paris. Wealth comes to us in several ways besides wads of cash—my wife inherited me. We cobbled together our sweat equity, planned carefully, had loads of help and a measure of luck, which proved sufficient to realize our vision of conquering France.

Coupled with zero adult supervision while young, I was an honorary orphan. That's not to say my mother didn't love me and work hard in a bingo parlor to keep a roof over our heads. But when my dad left for good in 1971, my older siblings, Vicki and Bill had already made their escapes and Pam—two years older than me—always had a chipper demeanor, which made me question if she really was a Piotter. That's when my mom and I both chased our comforts and drifted apart. What started as a celebration would last us both twenty plus years. Due to my mom's long suffering, she just didn't have the energy to care about details like what I did in school, what I was drawn to, or ran away from. At the start of our dueling two decades meltdowns, I enjoyed being on my own and wasn't much bothered by it. Gathering throwaways, I became a beacon for the unwanted.

Because my father was a classic narcissist and couldn't help but disparage my mom when they showed up together to visit me in prison, I made a choice to have no contact with him after I got out. Then there was the whole, him making fun of my brother Bill, while my brother was dying of AIDS thing. I finally got the memo on just how sick Bill Sr. was. He grew up with his own demons—a brutal father, and a mother who left him when he was a young teenager, then it was off to World War II and Korea. Not an excuse, only an explanation of what could've steered him mentally. I decided forgiveness and reconciliation are quite two different things and settled for the fraught memories instead.

My sister Pam did stay signed on to suffer his madness 'til the day he was put to rest. Bless her heart, Pam kept my whereabouts secret. He said to her, "Tell him he owes me money," before trying to borrow a large chunk from my sister Vicki, "to buy a piece of land so I can have something to leave my children when I die," he said.

Terrell and I have both spent half our lives working to quell our demons. Neither of us have children, not that we didn't want to, but by the time we met that ship had sailed. I know that if we had become parents together, she would've passed on her curious nature regarding all things art, beauty and healing. I couldn't have been graced with a more compatible partner. Anything I could say to express my love and appreciation for all she's given me wouldn't come close to being enough. I'm just sorry we didn't meet earlier. But alas, we were both ready when we were ready.

It's hard to write about the person I'm closest to. Others who know my wife may see her differently than I do, but here goes. When we met, I was about a month out of prison, terrified and excited by the prospect of exposing myself to someone. Someone who would get to know and see all of me, including flaws. Initially, I shared with her in a general way the extent of my self-inflicted psychosis, crime sprees and bottom feeder tendencies. She never judged and she never pried. She accepted and eventually loved me for who I was at that moment, and this. Twenty-three years ago, I viewed her as intellectually superior and brought forth from a proper place. Then she outed herself by laughing at my jokes. I know she's smarter than me and I've gained infinite knowledge from being in her presence. But my anti-education has also taught her a few things—cautionary tales.

I lost a testicle to a botched hernia operation when I was in prison. I was fairly twisted up about failure while presenting myself. In my mind, I was sure to fail. After a period of trial and error, she went with me to see a doctor. As it turned out, there was nothing physically wrong with me, my problem lay above the neck. I got my head screwed back on and our bodies have been very agreeable ever since.

We are both opinionated and often have spirited late night discussions, but we don't yell or say mean things and we don't go to bed mad. If ever a funky vibe enters our living space, laughter takes over to neutralize the threat.

As time passed, we got more comfortable with each other and I came to recognize what an extraordinary woman I had latched onto. There's nothing she can't imagine into existence. She's taught herself how to do so many things related to visual appeal. The morning after we got back from our first trip to France, I woke up to the sound of Terrell pulling our fireplace mantel off the wall with a prybar. She said, "I have aesthetic jetlag. I can't take it anymore." I admit, that 80's oak mantel was dowdy. Together, we built a flat, thick copper fireplace surround with beefy bronze barrel head screws for fasteners. Male urine will make a turquoise patina on copper and bronze. These are the type of facts she has tucked away for a rainy day. So I peed in a jar and poured it over the copper sheathing—outside—before installation. I also coaxed my dog Zinc to leave his mark. Together we created an exquisite effect.

My comfort has always been important to Terrell so she makes things we can't afford to buy. We live near Marché Saint-Pierre where there's an endless supply of fabric. She has built relationships with fabric sellers there and gets dibs on discounted Belgian linen. She started designing and making her clothes as a pre-teen, and since moving here has kicked it into high gear. In our Montmartre apartment, she's made everything—French pleat curtains, sheets, pillows, slipcovers, button down shirts with ancient mother of pearl buttons (hand sewing the button holes) dresses, pants, bathrobes, etc., etc. And beauty is always the achieved goal. When she latches onto an idea that requires my carpentry skills, I answer the call. Usually something to do with space management. There's no way to talk her down. And why would I? Only my lazy alter-ego would dare such a betrayal.

We are a sane and sober, legitimate family of two. Twenty-three years in and we couldn't love each other more. It's imperative to love each other living in such close quarters. I'd have followed her anywhere, but am grateful she chose Paris.

I was getting squeezed, so we built a 4' X 7' wood case on casters, to house Terrell's oversize paintings on paper.

Terrell is a multidisciplinary artist, envisioning blue chip status and a solo show at Le Centre Pompidou. She's created multiple series of paintings here in preparation. While she does all that, I swing a hammer, write and envision bookstore shelf space. I too, dream big. Head in the clouds, feet on the ground and all that. For two years, my first novel *Estrogen Rising* laid comatose under a cold, hard pile of rejection slips. After finishing two additional unknown entities I like to think of as books, it was time to put the paddles to Frankenstein's monster, grab it by the neck bolts and shake it up with another rewrite. Dismantle and reassemble to get it upright and lumbering towards publication. Sixty-five seems as good a time as any to break onto the scene, which doesn't appear to be a straight line.

I'd been holding my breath in anticipation of an unpublished fiction award announcement. When I saw the long list—one hundred twenty-eight names, people, and not one of them mine—I realized I've lived in towns less crowded.

My first thought was, *Are they nuts? Don't they know who I am? They don't?* Then, emotions rolled me up in a shame-blanket and took me away to an introverted humiliation hoedown, complete with fuck-it buckets to toss all my aspirations in. *I'll show them. I'll quit.*

I felt double fucked because I'd entered *two* books. After the storm blew over, I poked my head back out and had time to process. Just like that, I felt relief. I realized I wouldn't want to pitch my tent in such a torturous landscape waiting with the other insecure writers to get picked off, while the list got macheted down to seventy-five.

One novel I entered was short-listed for The Leapfrog Press (U.S.) and Can of Worms Press (U.K.) 2023 Global Fiction Prize. Eight names were on that list. Manageable. I'm happy to ride that *adrenaline rocket to nowhere* while I continue to query. Agents often include the question, "*What makes you the right person to write this book?*" Because I'm a person and I wrote the book? It used to be okay to make up stories while writing fiction.

If my dead dog Zinc was still alive and could read, he'd love my work. Three finished novels lie dormant on my desktop. I could have been making something tangible, like widgets, but instead, all I've got to show for ten-years of living inside my head is a thicker set of skin and two megabytes. The quest continues.

PREVISA, TWO MONTH RENTAL

Having sold the house on September 15, 2017, we moved the last of our belongings into storage, parked our vehicles at a friend's house and boarded a flight to France for a three-month, pre visa adventure. This time, two months in Paris, and a month in Provence. Roman philosopher Seneca said, "Luck is what happens when preparation meets opportunity." We were doing our part.

Prior to applying for visas, my wife and I were able to negotiate a two-month apartment rental through Airbnb, in part, because nightly rentals within Paris proper were officially dead. Those who chose to operate under the radar risked hefty fines from the city. Also, the apartment's owner liked the fact that we were so taken by France. She was pliant with her price point and we settled on a forty percent reduction from her unrealized nightly rate. Twelve hundred thirty euros per month for a semi-furnished three hundred fifty square foot apartment.

Jet lagged upon arrival, my response was, *"What the hell is this?"* What I had seen in the photos was a bathtub. What I saw for real was a small square shower that sat high above the floor to accommodate the above floor waste pipes, and a shower curtain hiding the fact that—that was some photographer—I'd been snookered. I threw a man tantrum. *"I'm not staying here,"* I said to my wife, who remained cool. She called an insightful friend, who said, "He'll get over it. What else is he going to do?" The nerve of that person having my number. I sucked it up. What else was I going to do.

In addition to providing us with a place to live, Madame Airbnb stepped in to help get us set up with a bank account, which was one of the high hurdles we were required to jump. She took a train from Burgundy with copies of her and her husband's documents in hand to provide to the bank and trusted we wouldn't steal their identities to lay claim to their cushy lives. She walked us to the copy center and told us to always copy documents in triplicate, knowing that, it may be overkill or maybe not. The absence of a tub suddenly seemed acceptable.

What our landlord did for us was also a leap of faith. She'd gone out on a limb by doing our bidding. As she marched us up to the bank to pass us off to another self-assured French female, she told us about a family of squatters—long gone, but still fresh to her senses. They cooked on a Hibachi, and it took her seven years to evict them. French law protecting tenants says no one can be put out from October through May. That's one reason it's so hard to rent.

Many expats we've recounted our experience to have blown a joy gasket, astonished at the warp-speed with which we got bank accounts. No small thing, even for the French. An American friend of a friend showed up in Paris to purchase an apartment. The deal didn't go through because she couldn't set up a French bank account. I'm talkin' bag-o-cash, people. A bank account is where the toe grabs French soil. With proof of a landing pad and our American bank records in hand—which showed we had a grace period before we'd need to be on the dole—we stopped by the bank to put this matter to rest.

I've heard many stateside speak of how snobbish the French are, especially Parisians. That's why I tightened my core at the bank, to deflect the blows. But there was no need. The truth is that just about everyone we encountered throughout this arduous process twisted themselves into pretzels to be helpful, and were happy to do so. D-Day lives. Lady Liberty *is* French.

Terrell and I have had countless guardian angels show up at make-or-break moments. Our landlady could only get us in the door, we'd still need divine providence to complete the task.

After the handoff at the bank, a young, take-charge male banker greeted us with a skewed smile which screamed, *Not today, Yankees.* He understood us to be Americans and was a little too generous with the finger wagging. While waiting, we watched as he sent an immigrant couple ahead of us packing. I wondered if French banks had a quota, like America's Highway patrol passing out tickets at the end of the month. I believe it was a testosterone thing, not a French thing.

In swooped Madame T., an imposing figure who sat higher up on the banker's throne. She informed him, "I'll take this one," and snatched us out of the jaws of defeat. He gathered his blank face and wobbled backwards, into obscurity. His obedience was without question.

We were ushered into the Queen's lair where she punished the keyboard with a furious barrage, hell-bent on silencing the alarm bells and squashing any potential disappointment. She regarded our perspiration and forehead wrinkles. She said, "No need to worry, I can get around this." After a fierce cyber battle, her digits of furry were not denied. She emerged victorious. For us, without Madame T. there would be no France.

She's since moved on to another branch and passed her ruby slippers off to a nice, helpful young man who indicated that if we ever needed a mortgage, he'd be there to help. Alas, it's been five years since I blew by the mortgage cut off period, so, no mortgage for me. In France they don't trust that at sixty something—beyond the French retirement age—I'd be able to pay it off. Hope this writing thing works out.

Three years after our first encounter with Madame T, we ran into her at a different bank branch. I remembered her as being at least six feet tall. She'd shrunk by a foot, but not by standing.

At that point our ninety-day no visa stay had run its course. We'd accomplished all we could have hoped for in advance of making our pitch, and it was back to the States to fret for four and a half months for a pre-visa freak out. Once our lodging and proof of bank account materialized in short order, we were ready to round up the other hundred-fifty-or-so documents necessary to make our case at the Consulate General of France in San Francisco.

Even though I no longer own the house in Seattle, I'm still getting cash offers beyond stratospheric. But hey, how can I regret what might have been for what is? I live in France, and you can't put a price on that.

As time has passed, our position in Paris has solidified and our social needle has moved from off our rockers to on the beam. Some of our friends have seen the light. Over seven years in, with the world again teetering, some are planning their own escape. A few are on their way. Two showed up today as I write this. In response to our forty-five reasons to ditch, some said, "I didn't think it would get that bad." I've always lived in the clouds, and even in my personal dark ages, I've pulled off some doozies—which I paid dearly for. So, moving to France did seem doable.

If timing is everything, according to 2018 world events, we hit a narrow window, like the ten-minute sweet spot of a perfectly ripe pear. In preparation for our big move, I searched the ethers for any leftover legal skid marks. Residue I'd not cleaned up from the swath of destruction I carved across the land as a young man. I didn't want to find out I was still contaminated while trying to make a clean break for it. Turns out, all I had to do was open my mailbox. It's strange because I hadn't been hiding from anyone.

The bottom shelf is still a shelf at Barnes & Noble.

A simple Google search would've produced my address, what I did for a living and for a fee, the promise of my juicy rap sheet for the purpose of extortion or public shaming. Because I have no shame, the dirt had already been spilled in the form of my buck-naked memoir, *Fixed, Dope sacks, dye packs and the long welcome back*, available on the very bottom shelf of your local bookstore. So, put your knee pads on to avoid carpet burns, get down on all fours and pick up a copy today. But, alas, the authorities finally found me. The skid mark showed up twenty-five years later.

I opened my mailbox to wailing sirens. I received notice that I owed for two rides to jail. One, in a comfortable, cootie-free police cruiser, with a price tag of five hundred fifty-three, interest-free dollars, for transport to my three hot's (*mostly roadkill*) and-a-cot *(far from natural latex)* at Grant County Jail in eastern Washington. Fair enough, I had no qualms about that, and gladly ponied up to make it evaporate and keep the blue lights flashing elsewhere. The other—same terrible year of living dangerously—to King County jail, with a price tag of twenty-seven hundred dollars. Nineteen hundred of which was an out-of-control, interest wildfire. Aside from the legal ramifications, rides in cop cars are expensive in Seattle. It was a bare bones '80s Dodge, for crying out loud. There weren't even any mind-altering goodies tucked between the seats. Believe me, I checked.

I wrote the sentencing judge and explained what a pillar of the community I had become since carving my swath of criminal destruction as a serial bank robber, so I could purge the streets of drugs and save America's youth. I asked if he had it in his heart to wave goodbye to the interest. Having already waved goodbye himself, he had no opinion.

He was dead.

But the Judge who stepped into his discarded black robe and swung the mighty, cherry-wood gavel of justice, did. The magical Magistrate agreed to waive his wand and put out the fire. He essentially said, "Go with God and don't ever come *the fuck* back." So—a shout out to Joni Mitchell—after being *raised on robbery*, I paid the eight hundred dollar cab fare and would soon be *a free man in Paris*.

I continue to flash back on how miraculously things played out. In March of 2017, when we first put our house on the market and I was convinced we'd be enjoying the spoils of a bidding war, but instead, got zero offers, I thought, *who are these lunatics who are not making offers on my pimped out 1980s mid-century, French-inspired knock-off*? Initially I'd been upset that it hadn't sold in March and when it did sell in August, upset that it didn't net *more* over the asking price. It's everyone's belief that their houses are worth way more money. What a bunch of ingrates I am.

Had we started the process earlier, one of the dominos may have fallen sideways. We might not have had such amenable consulate agents, secured an apartment, met the right people and so on. Our trusted friends assured us that as we get older, time becomes more valuable than money, and that we would make up the difference in short order after we planted ourselves. No sense in waiting for the perfect moment, a moment that may never come, was their take. Sage advice. So far, so good.

I was without a home, but not homeless and not adrift. Neither broke, nor broken and free to move about the planet as I pleased. Except to Canada, because Canada does not allow non-Canadians with criminal records to enjoy Canada. Money isn't everything, but it surefire took some of the sting out of couch surfing while we begged France to take us in. Offers to house sit in Seattle, in exchange for my mad skills as a Mr. Fixit started to roll in while we waited for an answer.

Chapter 7
Bugged Out

In February 2018, for our second housesitting gig, the beautiful Puget Sound view home appeared to be uninhabited. But first looks can be deceiving. I soon learned free is often expensive. Crater-clusters started to pop up and explode on my back, like bubbles in a flapjack. But it wasn't Job's nemesis God sending the messages, and I knew it wasn't shingles either because I'd been kicked by those viral mules before.

Could it be that such a stunning, well-kept property—one I'd remodeled and thought I knew well—was host to such devious, incognito eaters of men? As I sat watching the Seahawks game, popping boils like bubble wrap, I looked down. On the sofa's armrest, I spied a fat, comfortable, red translucent armchair quarterback, thrilled to witness Russell Wilson—pre-Bronco's misery—throw yet another touchdown pass. I connected the dots. You bet your sweet, blood sucking, parasitic, micro-crab ass it could.

Those monsters can stay dormant without protein for a whole year—kind of like I did during my fifteen-year cocaine safari—waiting for just the right lump of meat to show up hanging from the hook. I looked and felt like I'd been tenderized. Even my wife doesn't consider me that delectable. I'll never know how I rated that high on their picky pallet, but they had love only for me. My wife was spared. I had her all to myself.

The indignant owner's take was, "You must have brought them back with you from France." I doubted that, because why would any living thing voluntarily leave France? I scooped up the little porker and put it in a glass prison for further examination.

A trip to the clinic with suspect in tow confirmed what I already believed. The doctor hooked me up with a bedbug detecting beagle. Eager to please, the goofy detective worked tirelessly for treats. The pimp handler on the other hand, only accepted cash. He'd carved out a pretty good gig for himself enslaving that co-dependent treat-seeking missile. The duo came over and dug generations of skeletal remains—which had lived and died long before our arrival—out of the homeowner's mattress, sofa, and shag carpet crypts.

Ever since my wife and I got dragged by our first real estate agent—as a cautionary tale—through a house where shag carpet creeped halfway up the walls, and bible tracts and used condoms defiled the porch, I'm highly suspicious of shag carpet. Even in a pristine environment, it's enough to raise suspicion, neck hair and incentivize a gag reflex.

In addition to gas bombing the house, we took what was left of our belongings to the containerized fumigation site. A little sulfuryl fluoride never hurt anyone, we hoped. Again, we were homeless. So, we pounced on the offer to move back to my friend's condo directly under Seattle's Aurora Bridge, where we'd house sat the month before.

My wife made another plea. She called Paris to ask our two-month Airbnb host if she would consider holding her apartment open for us for a one-year lease until we got our French visas, and the cow jumped over the moon. She wanted to know what would happen if we didn't get visas and where would we live. The same two questions we'd discussed and gone over in our heads, ad infinitum, ones that we had no answers for and willed to go away. Were we descending into madness? If giddy qualified, then maybe.

She said, "I'll think about it." We offered to pay rent for the waiting period, to take her mind off the squatters, but being a true socialist, she waved the notion off. She said it wouldn't be right, that she'd talk it over with her husband and get back to us. A week later, she resigned herself to entertain our hallucination and hold the apartment until the stars aligned or fell out of the sky. Everyone involved leaned heavily on blind faith. We hunkered down in the fog bank to sweat it out. March 3, 2018, we applied online for French visas. Before flying into San Francisco to present ourselves, I purchased a monkey suit at Nordstrom Rack and a tie at the flagship store, to appease my fashion-conscious wife.

FÊTE-O-RAMA

Unlike me, the French have a full understanding of their country's celebrations. May goes slack with four four-day celebrations. Labor Day, May 1, WW II Victory Day, May 8, Mother's Day, May 25 and Ascension, May 29. Then comes the principal holiday for which the Republic stands, *Quatorze-Julliet. Fête Nationale,* or Bastille Day, France's Independence Day. The day the citizen-peasants, laborers and educated lower class had enough of having little say in government and paying taxes to the estates. So, they took ownership of the country by taking the political prison at Bastille on July 14, 1789. This resulted in the deaths of King Louis XVI and Marie Antoinette. Since King Louis XVI helped fund the American revolution ten years earlier, it could be said that he helped plant the French revolution seed. Without a head, I'll bet he didn't see that coming.

The Fire station in our neighborhood is spectacular.

Aside from all the live outdoor music, picnics and parades, one of the most beloved events is the fireman's ball. All over France, fire stations are open to the public to dance and drink with the *pompiers* (firemen). A celebration of the men and women who keep the country from burning and the citizens safe. I once became an honorary member of the Craig Alaska Fire department after I dropped an immense drunk, who lived above The Hill Bar, out a two-story window because of a fire he started in his apartment. I believe he was happy while saturated, because he considered the whole episode most amusing.

I went to the dance at the *pompier* station Napoleon opened in 1814. It is a Mansard building in the Marais, a former nobleman's house that was confiscated during the revolution and turned into the first fire station. The same station my nephew, Divisions Chief Cody Baker, of the South Kitsap, Washington Fire and Rescue Station, was given a personal tour of when he visited Paris. Cody doesn't speak French, but on that day, swapping photos in mutual admiration, they spoke each other's language.

Tonight is *Nuit des Musées,* museum night. All museums are free and open late in Paris, a bi-product of the revolution. It's also the seventh anniversary of our arrival here in France. I feel like it's a gift just for us.

Chapter 8
San Francisco Consulate

April, 2018. After crunching our way over the discarded syringes that littered the sidewalks, we were relieved that the good people in the employ of the consulate ran a tight ship. We stepped up to the window as the morning's first appointment. I watched while my wife navigated what seemed like a circus tent full of flaming administrative hoops. Thorough and efficient, she had all our paperwork numbered and in order. More of everything had been her motto. We said a little prayer.

Years earlier, I'd attended a Dress for Success seminar, which espoused the magic of the blue blazer. And for the first time, I got a chance to wear one. I was more used to wearing orange jump suits, so I was very proud. My blue blazer blazed, but the consulate staff never seemed to feel the heat.

We passed off the ultra-organized, two-inch thick stack of paperwork which included bank records, birth certificates, marriage license, school transcripts, business licenses, medical records, our French rental agreement and plane tickets—which at that time were required, whether they approved us or not—checking each item off the list. All present, accounted for, and in proper order.

I was dragged through a series of exercises very familiar to me. I sweated bullets as if it were a colorectal exam. I rolled my index fingers, my fuck you fingers, ring fingers, pinkies, and hitchhiking fingers (also known as thumbs), on the electronic ink pad, potentially forfeiting a future with my wife. Fortuitously, my impressive collection of self-inflicted felonies—possession of a controlled substance, second degree robbery of a 7-11 store with a socket wrench (which I turned myself in for), auto theft, a second second-degree robbery (which for a second time I turned myself in), because I was a dope fiend with a conscience, or an idiot, or both, depending on who chimed in. Then there was the grand finale that nudged me into retirement, eleven counts of bank robbery, for which I made them come and get me. It turned out that all of this happened before the International Crimes Database could cancel my reservation.

I waited while the inspector clacked away at the consulate keyboard, forgetting to breathe. My stomach roiled and I turned blue. While they processed my paperwork—in anticipation of a goon squad—I may have processed something myself. But praise be to deity, drop the confetti, I didn't have to pay twice. They found nothing, and I was officially a consideration.

The French policy wonks who accepted our mad stack from behind the bullet-proof plexiglass promptly flung our papers hither and yon across a two-meter slab of French oak. They asked us a few simple questions, "What do you plan on doing while in France?" came straight out of left field. *The fuck if I know,* blew in from Alcatraz. I was pinned down to come up with something with meat on the bones that wouldn't make me sound like a total knob, and leave them scratching their lovely heads of hair. I thought I might try funding socialism through the purchase of chocolate-infused bread. I needed an answer that would juice the rubber stamp and keep the line moving. To hypnotize, I flashed my paisley tie.

My wife presented her portfolio and gave her artist's elevator pitch without a hitch to synchronized head nodding. Next, I told the truth as I understood it at that moment. "Honestly, for a year, I don't want to do anything other than see the sights, study your beautiful language and write." When appropriate, a little brown-nosing never hurts. It proved pitch perfect.

The young woman said to me, "Why don't we put you down for a one-year travel visa?" It was the first indication that we were on the same side. That designation fit right in with my romantic notion of wandering the streets starry eyed, penning masterpieces on the fly, while dropping some serious change along the Champs-Élysées. Who wouldn't want to follow in the path of Hemingway, America's most famous expat writer ever, minus the whole booze and self-inflicted shotgun blast to the face, thing? *Is there a Costco on the Champs-Élysées?*

I got lost in thought about the Bay Area Book Festival I'd recently participated in. In the euphoric haze of having just published my first book, I booked half a tent on a street named *Radical Row*. My tentmate, the guy I shared the cost with, wrote a book titled: *Nazis and Nudists,* about Nazis and nudists. He assured me, "It's good." In preparation for my sale, I needed to order books from the printer. "How many?" I asked some trusted readers. The answer varied wildly. I landed in the middle, taking fourteen boxes of twenty-two books, three hundred eight in total.

I packed up the new Prius and headed south on Highway 101. My wife is a sober speed freak. She had that Prius doing 100 mph. When I pulled my nose out of a book I 'bout shit a brick. The Airbnb I'd booked resembled a toolshed, because it was a toolshed. One of twelve lined up in the backyard of a 1930's Craftsman. No windows. I said to my wife, "I'm no tool and I'm not staying in that cell." After raising holy hell and clawing back a refund from the indignant owners, my wife and I booked a room at a half-decent cheap-o motel near the venue.

I was surprised to see so many inebriants walking around with open containers so early in the morning at the bookish event. As the day progressed and the sun beat down, the crowd swelled to about ten thousand, give or take. The unpleasantness that stemmed from undelivered chemical toilets rose up like the oppressed.

My tentmate seemed to know a lot of antiquated weed hounds who sniffed about. Beat poets from yesteryear ducked into the tent to stoke a bowl. Since I don't partake, I left my post, desperate to escape the olfactory nightmare, only to be engulfed by the stench of urine. Day one, a total bust. On day two, hallelujah, the chemical toilets arrived—a victory in and of itself. It would be my only one. Two hundred eighty books would go home with me. People looked at me suspiciously as I gave them away like leaflets. A veritable laugh-riot, I sold six.

I snapped out of my flashback and said, "Yeah," to the consulate gatekeeper, "put me down for that," keeping in mind that it was only an application to be considered by the authorities in France. The whole experience went down like a Thanksgiving dinner. Days of preparation, fifteen minutes of power-eating, a couple hours to clean up, a night of tossing and turning, and a week to convince myself I never want to go through that again.

Wired from the emotional rollercoaster ride, we turned over our priceless passports and got ushered out to the waiting room, to squeeze by the remaining hand wringers who fretted over their futures. That was that. We snuck off down the streets of San Francisco.

LATE APRIL, 2018

Even though I grew up poor and without supervision, I understand that I've experienced privilege in my life. I was born white in a region of the world that would eventually prosper and have plenty of rich folk to steal from.

Fast forward. Being a homeowner in Seattle turned out to be a very good thing. Some people are born swaddled in bank notes. Some people start saving at a young age and build wealth slowly. *Pas moi*. Having been an insatiable dope fiend, which resulted in an extended stay at hotel hell, I bloomed late. But the crapshoot of life in the Pacific Northwest and the insane housing market—the same one that almost crushed me via foreclosure in 2009—jumped up to save my bacon. Thanks Jeff Bezos, *now pay your f-----g taxes.*

Giving up our cushy but uncomfortable lives and not knowing if we could get visas was a far-reaching leap of faith. When our beautiful ten-year project sold, we got a little bit closer. That moderate nest egg from the sale of our house took the sting out of homelessness and allowed us to make plans. We had already purchased our plane tickets, so there was no going back. Reality and doubt settled in. For a guy used to having an identity, I wasn't sure about anything anymore.

Having wrangled a one-year lease and French bank accounts, we were able to show the consulate gatekeepers in San Francisco what pit bulls we'd been, hoping it would bolster our position.

A week before our scheduled flight date to Paris we still had no confirmation that we'd been granted visas. We left the San Francisco consulate on April 24, and our plane was set to take off on May 16. We teetered but never toppled. We remained hopeful. I was still toggling between three construction jobs that had to be finished. Down to the wire on all fronts. I swung my bag of hammers like a contractor possessed, to set my mind free from the concept of failure. Having sold our house, we were officially priced out of the Seattle housing market and sure didn't want to hang around singing the blues if all the *crème* went sour.

Friday, May 11, my wife sent an email to our point person at the San Francisco Consulate, "Should we just cancel our May 16 flight?" We got a same day response from him, "*Got the clearance today. Unusually quick, you are lucky. I will print the visas and ship the passports today. Congratulations and bon voyage!*" We got our passports on Monday and would be in the air two days later. We really were headed to the haven of Lady Liberty's older sister on the banks of the Seine. Terrell got the artist's visa that, according to our paid consultant, required fame. Justice served.

I finished my three projects without cutting corners or any fingers. I got paid and again stored my truck and car, and flung the last of my belongings that hadn't found a home at anyone who could catch.

And then came a difficult task for me, something I knew would confront me at the very end. I gave all my power tools to my nephew, not because I'm a great guy, but because he is. And the fact that France doesn't have the same electrical set up. *"Who am I, if not a tool guy?"* I felt like I'd forfeited a small piece of myself. With all tasks but one ticked off the list, we were almost ready to board the plane.

When young, to capture the French vibe, Terrell made a beribboned Madame Pompadour dress in lavender gray satin. No stranger to big dreams, *sew it seems,* year after year, she wore that dress to the annual—why do I have to attend just because I'm the stupid husband—Halloween party, swearing she'd make it to Paris one day. The day before we got on the plane, we dropped that dress off at the Goodwill clothing collection box and that was that. I like to think somewhere in Seattle, a drag queen got dolled up. On May 16, 2018, we were up, up, and away on a plane to France with our seven, fifty-two pound suitcases packed to perfection.

Making contact with the 18th century and Clementine.

This is what we took with us to France. It would be four years until we shipped what was left of our belongings.

Chapter 9
Touch Down

After we landed as visa holders, Madame Airbnb called the gas and electric company to set up the bills in our names. A task that sends shivers through the spines of mere mortals, because French utility companies can be scary. Can-do women of a certain age are the backbone of French society. And this one was not one to be trifled with, as was evident by her command of the conversation. Gas, electric and phone bills are proof of residency and a necessary component that inched us closer to French social security numbers, being able to start businesses and secure what the French call the open sesame, the *Carte Vitale*—socialized medical cards.

Fall, 2018: All new arrivals are required to contact the *préfecture de Police* website and set up a face-to-face meeting within ninety days to get an identity card with visa status. In an attempt to formalize our assigned designations, many appointments we made directed us to the same building, but for different reasons, which made us think we'd taken care of things we hadn't. Even the authorities were hard pressed to explain why.

This was my wife's turn in the French bureaucratic barrel, mine was still a few chewed fingernails away. She was tasked with tracking down where to go to get the long stay talent visa she made her pitch for in San Francisco. France gifted her the talent visa but didn't tell her where to cash in when she got here. Newly elected President Macron had widened the talent visa to include academics, scientists, etc. This created a need for an additional office for processing, but no one could tell us where it was. It was a bit of a treasure hunt.

I've never been one to seek the company of police, but I noticed the laid-back demeanor of the *gendarmerie*, whose absence of steroid-induced bulging neck veins put me at ease. We went to the nearest station and asked a chill, blue uniform, *"Excusez-moi, où allons-nous?,* where do we go?"

He said, "Not here," with confidence. He pointed to a dot on a map, kilometers away. "You must go to *this* police station to register. *Au revoir."* We crisscrossed the city, burning through Metro tickets like Snoop Dog burns spliffs, while being told, "Not here" over and over.

After introducing ourselves to the entire Paris police force, we discovered that the correct, spankin' new office was only two doors down from where we'd started. The sign on the door read, "Closed for the day."

When it did open, my wife and I were presented with temporary paper copies, known as *récépissés,* of our prospective visas. Hers, a two-year talent visa, and mine, a one-year visitor visa. They would let us know via email when to pick up the laminated copies. I was questioned why I hadn't signed up for a family member visa—*hitched myself to my wife's artist's-visa-wagon?* I said, "Nobody told me, *podna."* The prefecture's visa stud explained that it would allow me to work or not work, whatever floated my *bateau*. It's what my wife called the Golden Goose visa. I viewed it as the leisurely gateway to prosperity. Being an annoying American knockabout until my money ran out really didn't interest me. Within five minutes my possibilities expanded. I walked out of the prefecture in Paris with a two-year visa and a glow. I was no longer a slacker. I was husband of wife, and future money maker. I had time to sort out what might become of me. The magnitude of what had just happened was lost on me. In short, I'd been granted permission to work and make my own way in a new country. All I had to do was find a job. Yikes!

PARIS CALLING

Our rental sat high up in Paris's Belleville, in the 19th Arrondissement, just off the Pyrénées Métro line 11, a working-class neighborhood with heaps of charm, not so far from Père Lachaise cemetery. It was a stand-alone city until it got folded into Paris proper in 1860. The park at Buttes-Chaumont, just a block away, was built on a defunct limestone and gypsum quarry that helped build a good chunk of Paris. It is sixty-one acres of urban bliss with a vista view of the city. It has a cave with a waterfall, a Roman cupola, rolling hills, exotic trees. One can experience the sound of Arabic women's joy cries, see a pandemonium of parrots, a murder of crows and the occasional puppet show. And like the parrots and crows, people of all stripes flock there for a respite. There's a lake fed by two streams from the Bassin de la Villette and a suspension foot bridge anchored into the stone.

Down the block and up seventy-five steps, sits Butte Bergeyre, a surreal oval-shaped village of stand-alone Art Deco houses with a striking view of Montmartre across the valley. It's separated from the noise and traffic below, a city within the city. In 1918, a soccer stadium that accommodated fifteen thousand screaming fans was inaugurated, and exactly 100 years before the 2024 Paris Olympics, it was put to use for the 1924 Paris Olympics. In 1926, it was razed because of maintenance costs due to its instability. Developers swooped in with backfill and gypsum scraps from Butte Chaumont's quarry to create a base for construction of the village. One of the many oddities I've stumbled upon while nosing around.

Today, the park is safe, but not so long ago not a place you'd want to be when the sun went down. Pre-park days, the soil was *so* toxic, there was zero vegetation, hence the name *Chauve-Mont* or bald hill. Being close to the slaughterhouses, it's where workhorse carcasses—waste not want not—were dumped after slaughter and criminals were hanged for public viewing. Something for the whole family to do before Netflix.

There is virtually no air conditioning in Paris apartments, only store bought portables which sell out in a flash. The old buildings in Paris are oppressively hot in the summer and there's no escaping the heat, especially those facing south. During the 2019 seven-day heat wave where temperatures hovered at 107º Fahrenheit, the city opened the park all night so the neighborhood residents could sleep outside.

Week one, surveying the street from our second-floor walk-up—in France, the first floor is one up, second, two up and so on—I spied a string of limos creeping down Avenue Simon Bolivar, with horns and music blaring. Happy Saturday, a wedding was in progress. Bentleys are quite the ride, but not fireproof. There was a loud pop and a plume of smoke followed by flames that built momentum and raged from under the hood. Pyrotechnics and part of the show? Apparently not. For a time, the music hung in there. The driver stopped the procession and along with the bride and groom, bailed out to ponder. Seemingly unperturbed, the passengers remained in a celebratory mood. The car was given space to burn all the way to the ground. I was surprised to see what little was left in the aftermath.

No one seemed alarmed except me and the firemen. Even though I'd spent two months in the neighborhood prior to moving there, I was so focused on not getting lost that I'd missed out on many of its features. I thought, *this could be an interesting neighborhood.*

Two days after the Bentley blazed, the universe sent me a reminder. Looking out my window, I witnessed a party in full swing across the street. I thought, *man doesn't that look like the place to be,* until a guy fell out of his own second story window. Alcohol blurred his senses and a compromised balcony railing finished him off. The ambulance showed up within a couple of minutes, but once there dawdled. In due course, they covered him up and puttered away. Then I thought, *shit goes sideways in this neighborhood, I'd better keep on my toes.* It's only natural that those two incidents had me bracing for another neighborhood calamity.

Up the street, on the other end of the bummer spectrum, was a café with decent coffee and the best little wire baskets full of frites. The day was chilly and the clouds were indecisive, but inside the café was bustling. I was at the jam wagon outside the café, where a woman hawked her out-of-this-world home-made confitures. A *petit camion* (little truck) screeched to a halt out front, indicating something important was about to happen.

The driver jumped out, slapped down a half sheet of plywood on the sidewalk in front of the entrance and produced a starburst acoustic guitar. A lean, middle-aged Latina appeared from the passenger side wearing a flame-red dress, with ruffles trailing down the side, sturdy red heels and a red, wide-brimmed felt hat. Accompanied by her driver/guitarist, she launched into a blistering athletic dance routine, unleashing a barrage of exquisite improvised syncopation. She snapped out Afro-Cuban rhythms with castanets, then hitched up her dress to go to work on the plywood, firing on all cylinders. As a drummer I was awed. The café's patrons stampeded the door, climbing over each other to witness the miracle of her explosive presence, which left us all breathless. Her axe man was no joke either.

After raucous applause, she passed her Cordobés hat, then piled in the truck with her damaged plywood and maestro partner, and peeled off down the rue, to wow the next crowd. I'd never seen impromptu like that in Seattle. It was five minutes I'll always remember.

Thursday nights, a few doors down, a jazz café offered the resurrected voice of the Little Sparrow, Edith Piaf, accompanied by the ghost of Miles Davis—here, known as Kilometers Davis—to fill the night air. There's a plaque nearby, at 72 rue de Belleville which states: "Edith Piaf was born in destitution on the steps of this house on December 19^{th,} 1915. Her voice would later greatly move the world."

As a counterbalance to the afore mentioned burning of the Bentley—which my neighbor assured me was *n'est pas grave*, (no big deal)—a string of national pride evoking events took place shortly thereafter. *Les Bleus*, France's National football team (round footballs, y'all) won the

World Cup. There was so much viral joy, wonder and excitement, I thought I might explode. A lot of alcoholics and babies were conceived on that weekend. Everybody loved everybody and then some. The whole kissy face thing was taken to absurd levels. Due to Covid—talk about withdrawal symptoms—that activity stopped abruptly and all were forced to learn the elbow bump as a stand-in.

Fête de la Musique happens every June 21, during the summer solstice and is another reason that I love France. All caliber and variety of musicians, and the citizens of every city, town and village pour into the streets to play, dance and drink, pulsating into the wee hours. All over France, music is alive and well. It's an infusion that directly feeds my soul.

Chapter 10

Only Sick Above the Neck

In the cheek by jowl scrum of Paris's thirty-three square miles, one never knows what manner of being they might bump up against. Upon arrival, newbies of all ilk are lumped together as a fraught, wriggling mass of perplexity. Akin to a litter of puppies—eyes still closed and hungry to understand the outside world.

The government-approved clinic's waiting room is where foreign nationals' hearts flutter to the notion of passing physical muster as potential residents of France. Whether an able-bodied, budding-socialist just one financial blip away from being sent packing like me, or a birth lottery winner eager to spend the pile down and pass on the crumbs to their spawn before ditching this smoldering orb, all are illuminated under the government's microscope to ensure they won't leak any funky contagions on the ruddy-cheeked population. Also, insurance against any shipping costs anchored to corpse or casket. The good news is, if one does retreat via pine box, they'd be sent back duty-free and beat the tax man one last time. This is how I fret while waiting to be sized up.

In a seat too short, wondering, *Where am I supposed to put the rest of my ass,* I struck up a conversation with a stately African gentleman in the spartan seat next to me. Still jazzed from having just landed, I came off a bit full-throated. Mentoring in a lower tone, he told me he'd climbed the ladder of success to the position of head of state for one of France's colonial entanglements. I studied his hands for calluses before realizing his climb had been symbolic.

He said he'd been deposed—the victim of a coup d'état—and that, in his part of the world, a steady stream of presidents fell by the wayside. I viewed his presidential declaration as suspect. He could've just been having a little fun with a nobody who he'd never see again, though I had no doubt he'd had good reason to flee.

In a bygone era, I tossed out plenty of my own whoppers. I told a guy who was also waiting to be sentenced to prison, "I invented the Weed Eater, but someone stole my idea." I shook my sack lunch at him, "Hence, the baloney sandwich." I was just relearning how to read and fancied ten-dollar words to sound important. My tactic didn't move the status needle in the land of dereliction. The implausibility of my bold statement made me feel about as dignified as my upcoming delousing via chemical shower. My compadre, obviously out of the Weed Eater loop said, "That's raw. Why didn't you just smoke it?"

Mr. potential ex-President inquired about me. I told him the truth, that other than love, curiosity and the avoidance of flat-earthers, there was no logic behind my mad, five thousand mile dash to the haven of France. I wasn't 100 percent sure why I'd sold my house, dumped the rockin' business I'd spent years building out of blood and Band-Aids to follow my wife to a land where nobody laughed at my jokes and my tongue slipped into a coma. And, if I failed my physical, I'd be on the streets and forced to learn how to play a second-hand accordion.

Something had grown inside me I couldn't put my finger on, but is probably listed in *The Diagnostic and Statistical Manual of Mental Disorders*. Craving commiseration, I'd muscled myself onto his imaginary sofa. Unflappable, he offered only nods and barely audible grunts. I felt exposed and flaked off, like Forest Gump at a bus stop.

I'd yet to solidify my position and build my manic confidence muscle. I'd had plenty of convictions but not enough conviction. A shadow of doubt leeched in. I teetered. He on the other hand, lacked my lack and seemed to know exactly why he'd fled. I had to believe if he was who he said he was, France would be obliged to prop him up in some form or fashion. A you break it, you own it type situation.

Later that day, I asked the Global Organization of Oriented Group Language of Earth, (GOOGLE) if I'd managed to make noodles out of his raw lump of truth. *Et voilà!* There Mr. President was on my screen, looking solemn and every bit presidential, as though the weight of the world rested on his capable shoulders. A second, pixelated image formed in my head. *A hunted leader on his way out.* He'd been straight up with me.

He also told me the military leaders didn't deem him greasy enough to lube the perpetual grift cannon that shot his nation's assets straight to the top military brass, so out he went. I'd never met a president before, but I *did* get a formal reply for a letter I'd written to President Obama for saving my home through his Making Home Affordable Act, and my sister *did* deliver mail to the rock band, The Presidents of the United States of America.

On that day, Mr. President, like me, was at the mercy and temperament of the underpaid, stethoscope-toting white lab coat zombies, who asked me, "So, how's that Hep-C doing?" which snapped me back to reality. A fair question—fallout from my madcap needle jabbing days—seeing as how they, too, felt compelled to tap my veins for information. The speed with which they processed was on par with corn through a goose. I could almost smell my own trepidation.

"Oh that," I said, and handed over the readied report from my U.S. family doctor. I never understood medical mumbo jumbo, especially since I never read it. But *mon Dieu!* It turns out the French lab coat *did* read and understand medical gibberish, even in English. His team then compared the charts with my freshly spilled blood and deemed me salvageable.

Seems I still had enough liver function left in the tank to hustle forty percent of every euro I gathered for the government coffers and was only still sick above the neck. Mr. President, I suspect, disappeared down a bourgeois booby-hatch connected to the Rive Gauche, where he'd be allowed to live semi-large and reasonably safe, in obscurity.

TENACIOUS T.

After getting flaked off by a naysaying government automaton, Terrell hunkered down on the travertine tile on the wrong side of Maison des Artiste's door. The big *fromage* finally showed up with a wad of keys dangling, and a furrowed brow. He inquired, "What, Madame, are you doing?" Tenacious T. made her plea, "I'm here to apply for a Social Security number," one of the multi-digit numbers required to be somebody in France.

The boss said, "You must apply online."

T. said, "That's what Madame told me." She began to explain one of the many circuitous bureaucratic conundrums, "your web site requires me to enter my Social Security number in order to make an appointment. I'm trying to find out how to *apply* for a Social Security number." Terrell visited about every government building in her quest. Immigrating is not for weenies. Her desire and common sense exposed the crack in their system's reasoning. He rubbed his chin, acknowledging her dilemma, and bent the rules with three sweet words, "Come with me."

THE FRENCH TAX AUTHORITY

After making an accounting blunder and being summoned by the ominous French tax authority, *Impôts*, I was given a bit of advice by a native

Parisian, "Wear a tattered sweater, drag a foot and broken or not, put a piece of tape on your glasses. Present your best, pathetic self. Just try to look sick, anything to throw them off the scent." It sounded like an old tactic I used to squeeze the State of Washington out of a few bucks back in my using days, except then, I really was pathetic.

I said, "Hmmm." Once in the office, I looked around. It did appear to be a popular ploy designed to conjure pity and circumvent debtor's prison—as was apparent by all *les thespians* foot dragging around the lobby. I dressed for success, because to me, what was suggested sounded more like work than paying my fair share. Plus, they don't take pity, they take euros.

Impôts is equipped with a digital vacuum, connected to all business and personal banks accounts, ready to hoover at the touch of a button. When money is due, they will not be denied. Unless the funds have been spent, in which case they put a lock on the offender's bank account, which—I hear tell—is an expensive and disruptive proposition.

Impôts strikes fear, so when they offered me an opportunity to explain and make things right, I lunged at the opportunity. I told them I went on the site, filled out the forms, declared my income, clicked pay, then paid, and showed them a screen shot of the receipt.

They said, "That's not a receipt, you missed a few steps." They also do everything in triplicate digitally. I'm happy to say, we worked it out and I'm currently current.

Now, in my sixth year as a business owner, I've come to realize France is in dire need of a webmaster. There are many secret portals one's expected to know how to duck in and out of on *Impôt's* website. France offers a three-year grace period for first-time business owners, which means I wasn't required to add a surcharge on my wages to pass along to the Republic.

I started my business in August 2019, but the first seven months of that year counted against my three years. No one—accountant, government, acquaintance, sooth sayer—told me. I was required to claw back from a client, a twenty percent surcharge above what I charged for my services for seven months of work and send it to the tax authority. A sizable chunk. Month by month it seems to get more complicated. I've come to find out that that twenty percent surcharge is only supposed to be ten percent for residential remodeling. This I was told by an American client/attorney of mine who specializes in research. Information not freely given on *Impôt's* website. Hence, the need for a webmaster. I'm not complaining, this is what I signed up for. This is socialism.

Not knowing the details generates fines, and not knowing about fines generates fines. The layered system of entry into the paperwork labyrinth has caused many super-humans to pack it in, five minutes before the epiphany.

A LITTLE ABOUT THE BANKING SYSTEM

I can tell you that with no tellers or cash drawers in France, bank robbers here have it rough. And if tellers did hold cash, during Covid it would've been tough to differentiate between someone making a legitimate withdrawl and someone like me who was unauthorized. I might've have thought, *Are they all in line to rob the bank?*

It's been my experience that in France, banks march to their own rhythm. I got a message from BNP, my bank of eight years that said, *Welcome to your new branch!* They'd moved my account to a town I'd yet to discover, kilometers outside of Paris. The catalyst was that I ordered a package of checks, so naturally they needed to close my account and give me the boot. When I asked why all my money had been transferred to a branch in Butt Crack Nowhere, the maniacal bank clerk pulled up my info, clacked away at the keys and told me I needed to make an appointment at my new branch to get my question answered. I looked around for someone who was firing on more than one cylinder. I saw no one, but I did hear two others crunching snacks and bandying banter in the shadows.

A friendly face emerged who I'd interacted with before. I pounced and quickly spilled my indignation. She intervened on my behalf, waived the appointment I was to make and told her colleague, "Quit pressing the keyboard." Then presto, I was once again worthy of parking my money at my neighborhood branch. My checks never did show up. I went back a week later to thank her again, but she too had been transferred to a different branch—wouldn't want any continuity.

Shortly after that episode, my debit card was set to expire in three weeks, so I ordered a new card. The bank said it would be in my mailbox in ten days. I said, "Please don't cancel my debit card until the new one comes. I'm going on vacation Monday and will need access to my account."

They said, "Of course, we wouldn't do that." Based on their track record, I withdrew a wad of cash, just in case. I don't think they even waited until I got out the door to cancel my card. When I got back and called them on it, their response was, "*C'est bizarre.*"

STEADY STREAM OF VISITORS

Once settled and lit up by the City of Lights (the most visited city on the planet), I started getting periodic messages like this from people I vaguely remembered: "Hey friend, I'm coming to Paris," or "Hey friend, my friend, niece, neighbor, fill-in-the-blank is coming to Paris. Wouldn't it be great if you could hang out with them or them or them?" I used to lunge at the notion.

Veteran transplants cautioned, "They'll grind you down and spend your discretionary energy. Some have no interest in you, they'd be calling anyone they knew who lives in Paris. What they propose is code for, 'Will you be my tour guide slash bi-lingual babysitter, so I can escape the embarrassment of looking like an American while trying to order a baguette?' Unless they're dear to you and you love them, you've got to be firm or they'll take over your life." Looking back at all those days I never got to live for myself, I now consider the concept of no as enlightened.

Tourists' agendas are generally so jam-packed they're impossible to achieve without a jet pack. *Sorry, not available,* became my standard, three-word reply, met with resounding silence. That's not to say I haven't carved out generous chunks of time to show off this beautiful city to genuine friends and loved it, but I'm in my last chapter and for maximum value, need to spend down what's left wisely.

Dining in our neighborhood park with my dear friend Phil. He's made the journey to come see us from Seattle three times. We had a hell of a time keeping the food from sliding off the table.

Chapter 11
Un Peu de Puissance

When dealing with an apathetic customer service rep, *Excusez-moi de vous déranger (*excuse me for disturbing you) is one of the French phrases that nets results. My acknowledgement that I'm a bothersome foreigner straightens spines, perks up ears and turns indifference on its head. They often become so helpful I sometimes wonder how to turn off the cheer spigot so I can go back to being a semi-clueless dweeb. But every so often, there sits an acerbic wonk not even willing to meet me on the border of what's reasonable.

For a second time, my wife and I were forced to suffer at our landlord's beautiful 18th century manor house in Burgundy, near the Yon River Valley, where a cluster of Napoleon's soldiers took shelter and carved their names in the oak rafters before serving up some more of Napoleon's whoop-ass. The first temporary eviction was because Madame had double-booked by scheduling an Egyptian couple for a ten-day stay before we knew of our visa status. The second was when she scheduled work on our apartment's ceiling because of a water leak from above. In both cases I give her props. She did her best to accommodate everyone involved.

After my plastic identity card arrived, I noticed they'd spelled my middle name Berry, not Barry. No big deal. I let it ride, but every time I looked at my card and saw *Berry*, it gnawed at me. Still tainted with the habit of telling on myself, I decided it best to let the authorities know and possibly get a French attaboy. Wrong. What kind of international crisis was I trying to create? Stop the visa presses. Suddenly, my status was in jeopardy. They required me to provide additional paperwork. Many face-to-face bureaucratic tasks happen impromptu, so they said, "Check your email, we'll let you know what to bring, when to bring it, and where." I thanked them for the specifics.

A windmill in Burgundy.

Chillin' on the Yon River, one hundred miles outside of Paris, my email wasted no time in blowing up. "HEY BARRY, GET YOUR ASS BACK HERE RIGHT NOW!" I scrambled to get the stack of papers together and make the early morning train. Alone. My wife said, "You'll need to take *all* the documents." Being a case-hardened know-it-all, I said, "No, I don't. I only need *these* documents," and flapped a stack of second-string paperwork. *What am I, an idiot?*

At the Paris office reception desk, I saw the personable young man pass by who'd been responsible for botching my middle name on my initial visit. When I stepped up to present myself to the woman behind the counter, I used my fail-proof and grammatically incorrect phrase, *"Excusez-moi, ma français ce n'est pas très bon."* Bad moon rising—the stone-faced gatekeeper's expression only got worse. She looked through my scant stack and said, *"Non,"* and tried to brush me aside like a flakey fungus. But I did not give right of way to her next victim. I tried to bend her to my will, which would have taken Uri Geller type skills to pull off. The volume between us ratcheted up. I held my ground. She summoned security. It felt like jail was just around the corner. I prayed for divine intervention. Just then, the young man again floated my way. So I glommed onto him and spilled the situation faster than it would've taken for security to gaffle me up.

I'd left a vital piece of paperwork, with an official Government stamp which would prove I'd paid the fee. The piece my wife suggested I take. My bad, y'all. He commiserated.

Madame Misery *perdu sa merde* (lost her shit). It was a pivotal moment. I envisioned calling my wife from jail, waiting to be deported and preparing for life as a bachelor. I clung to my savior. The nice young man so appreciated my humiliation, he called off the dogs and ushered me into his office, where I was given a mulligan. It was a crushing defeat for the stickler seething behind the desk. Whoop, whoop, I win again! She was furious I'd gone over her head to get my needs met.

I called my wife from his office to confirm my idiocy. She scanned and sent the missing document and the parade resumed inside my little victory bubble. I *was* required to go back out, face my abuser and wait for her to ink a signature. I'd also have to take whatever blows my wife rained down on me, later. Young man swallowed hard, gave me a nudge and said, "Good luck."

Seems Madame's ink well had temporarily run dry. After three hours—the time it took forty-eight thousand babies to enter Earth's fray—it was time to close up shop. That's when I got the required signature and permission to get G.T.F.O.

Even *before* Covid hit, Paris got dragged through a wringer. There were the *gilets jaunes*, or yellow jackets. What started as a peaceful protest about a gas tax, morphed into a raging river of young, angst-ridden man-children pining for a revolution. They seemed bent on disfiguring any business along the Champs Elysée, or any other hifalutin street that didn't fit into their narrow scope of acceptable capitalism.

The French adventurer, Sylvain Tesson put it best: "France is a paradise inhabited by people who think they're in hell." I would modify that statement by saying, *some people*. When I was leaving an event at the American Church with a friend, a scrum of wannabe revolutionaries along the Quai did have the decency to pause and address us in the formal. They said, *"Bonsoir Monsieur-dame,"* ceded a path away from the mayhem, then resumed smashing car windows. I speak from experience— there's a lttle bit of good in the worst of us.

Once everything was sufficiently wrecked and they got their nihilist's stamp of approval, it was back to mom and pop's manor house, for prepared meals, laundry service and allowance. I can tell you for certain it wasn't the North African immigrants busting the joint up.

At least if they hurt themselves while vandalizing, they'll benefit from socialized health care. One would think that with all the free education floating around, they'd find a better solution to what ails them than destroying other people's property.

Next came the Metro strikes, a carefully scheduled series of minimally-disruptive shutdowns. One strike started on May 1, a national holiday, but not until 9:00 am after I'd already taken the metro across town. On the long walk home, I stumbled upon the gilded statue of Joan of Arc on Rue de Rivoli. A large crowd had gathered for a speech. I asked an English-speaking Frenchman, "What's going on?"

He vehemently spit out, "Old man Le Pen is rallying his troops."

I said, "Eww." For some reason, the French far-right gather and whack off to the image of the Joan of Arc on a horse to suit their delusional nationalist agenda.

Then, the biggest blow to the country's identity, the fire at Notre Dame, known as Point Zero, the center of the country and the birthplace of France. Based on the sheer volume of tourists, it's evident to me that Paris is the center of the known universe.

Then came Covid, and the 2023 sanitation worker's strike. I used to wonder, *how much garbage can a city like Paris produce?* Now I know.

HEFTY! HEFTY! HEFTY!

In March of 2023, half of Paris got buried under a mountain of rubbish. The other half retained its usual perfumy urine smell, untouched and business as usual. The city sanitation workers took a stand against President Macron's proposed increase of the general public's retirement age from sixty-two to sixty-four and sanitation workers' retirement age from fifty-seven to fifty-nine. I'm a sixty-five-year-old construction worker with seven years to go so I can claim full benefits in America, *if they still exist*. I doubt if I went on strike here I'd have much of an impact. I hear that in the U.S. there are ninety-year-old greeters at Walmart. *Welcome to Walmart, welcome to death.*

Of the twenty neighborhoods in Paris, ten are serviced by city workers who chose to strike, the other ten by contract workers who chose not to. My neighborhood, Montmartre, along with nine others, was not affected by the strike and remained pretty much pristine. In the ten that were affected, pyramids of garbage created funky building facades with only the doorways exposed. Corridors of garbage were built on the sidewalks with just enough room for a skinny Parisian to squeeze through.

One of my French friends said, "The rich neighborhoods have it the worst because they eat a lot of seafood. Shrimp tails do not age well." Holy Mother of God were those neighborhoods stanky. For three plus weeks I barely left my 'hood. Mayor Anne Hidalgo was asked to do something. To paraphrase, she said, "It is not my place to do something, they are exercising their right." *Vive Anne!*

Rat birth rates exploded during the strike and the restaurant trade fell off a cliff. People didn't want to eat surrounded by garbage. And if rats made their way in for a seat at the table, health inspectors would be working overtime shuttering restaurants—both major concerns that turned the tide in the negotiations. There's generally a lot of horn honking in the streets of Paris, but it's never directed towards garbage trucks. Sanitation workers are revered, so the public, though inconvenienced, stood by the heroes of Paris. In the end, the retirement age did get raised, along with plenty of French hackles.

Chapter 12

Construction Sherpa

After seventeen months of furious scribbling in cafés, leisurely strolls through le Jardin des Tuileries, language school, and wandering aimlessly to metabolize the city—with only my stomach to tell me the time—my American work ethic started to guilt trip me into submission. There are a lot of bridges on the river Seine and I didn't aspire to live under any one of them. It was time to go to work.

Three times a week, on my way back from Alliance Française language school, I walked by what is considered the birthplace of France, Notre Dame cathedral on Île de la Cité. On April 15, 2019, I was standing in front of the gothic cathedral in awe, not an hour before the fire raged that consumed the roof's original framing—known as the ancient forest—lead roof skin and oak spire. The city was on edge. Église Saint-Sulpice, a Rive Gauche cathedral—its exterior featured in the film, *The Da Vinci Code*—had caught fire a month before with minimal damage. Ron Howard wasn't allowed to film inside, so he had his own Saint-Sulpice built in a London movie studio. It seems the church heavyweights were chapped by the swarm of pagan visitors. A statement they hung in the church read: "Contrary to fanciful allegations in a recent bestselling novel, this is not the vestige of an ancient pagan temple."

My friend Bruno, a veteran war correspondent, temporarily hit pause with all the war business—until the Ukraine war exploded on the scene—to report on the softer side of life. He'd just interviewed the Directrice Générale of the Historic Monument Society, whose duties include hiring the renovation crews for all things France. Granted, having just turned fifty-nine the day before the fire broke out didn't make me stand out as a must hire, but I am fit, knowledgeable and wanted to contribute towards the rebirth of Our Lady.

My wife is a big believer in the power of the resume, in French and English. She poked at me to put both on paper. I've experienced the value of documentation—like, not losing my house to foreclosure—and have a large body of work from yesteryear, so it was relatively easy to park the pastries, and get off my tuchus to put together a reasonable CV. I made my pitch, in French, to work on Notre Dame. Here's the gist of my heartfelt letter.

Chère Madame Secrétaire Générale,

Grovel, grovel, smooch, smooch, lickety-bum. And a litany of other brown-nosed supplications geared towards my vision of glory and a plot at Père Lachaise. Despite all the supplication, my letter to the goddess of French monument rehab didn't grab Madame Secrétaire Générale's full attention, so I struck out swinging. It did move my thinking away from perpetual slacker and towards being a full-fledged taxpayer in the euro-zone. The way I'd been burning money I needed to be in the euro zone. The process had been the point. Pitching myself turned out to be a great confidence builder and prepped me for more opportunities to come.

After my rejection, I was pounding the cobblestone streets of Saint-Germain-des-Prés when I noticed a sign for what is the equivalent of a Carpenter's Union. This led me to the *Chambre du Commerce* and one of my guardian angels.

My wife, who I'd relied heavily on to navigate the language portion of the program, declined my generous offer to babysit. Alas, I was forced out of the crib to brave bureaucracy on my own. By this time, I'd scabbed together a mental rolodex of bastardized phrases. A five-year-old's—me hungry, foreign tongue butcher—kind of knowledge, without conjugated verbs. Just enough to be understood and provide amusement to the locals. So, I took my intestinal fortitude, my glossy catalogue, plus my spiffy new resume, written in *French*, down to the *Chambre du Commerce* with the goal of strutting out a big baller, shot-caller business owner.

The office is—as it should be—run entirely by women. Hooray for me, I am a feminist who envisions a world run by strong women. Even though for much of my childhood I was estranged from my mom, I've always been a momma's boy and believe women to be more level-headed than men. Women certainly aren't responsible for the mess we all find ourselves in. My wife confirms my belief every day. She says if she ran the show, she'd drop estrogen bombs and then everyone would want to tidy up.

The capable gatekeeper sat me down, groovin' on my gibberish. She told me I was required to have three-year's experience working for a French company before I'd be allowed to form my own company. A crack formed in my chutzpah. I told her I'd only been in France for seventeen months, so the math didn't add up. I closed my eyes and thrust my portfolio at her. I shared with her my desire to pay taxes in a country not beholden to a military industrial complex and that uses their collection box to take care of its people.

She said, "Many self-employed citizens have an aversion to paying taxes and choose to live in the black." Meaning, live under the radar as cheats. She said, "You would be in the minority." I can confirm her statement based on the trembling masses called to the carpet in the tax authority's office.

Madame poured over my glossies and some positive noises started to leak out. She said, "Just a minute, I'll have to ask the big boss." She took my folder and disappeared, leaving me to write a dystopian horror story in my head. She came back five minutes later with the keys to my future. "The big boss says yes." *Long live France!* They rubber stamped me. She ushered me to the V.I.P. lounge, sat me down and spent three hours manipulating the bureaucratic-beast-machine while feeding it my specs.

She asked the universal question, "Mother's maiden name?"

I answered, "Monsarrat."

She lit up and about levitated out of her chair. "*You are French!*" she proclaimed. It prompted her to clack the keys with a little something extra. This divine being—the third French female superhero to show up in my path—is largely responsible for my expedited status in France and the ability for me to earn a living. I reiterated, "I really do look forward to paying taxes."

Because I started working and happily paying taxes, when Covid-19 hit and I was apartment bound, the French government tapped into their emergency fund to take care of me financially until it was safe to go back to work. Some expats I've talked with play the victim and consider French bureaucracy an enemy out to punish them with excessive charges. With all its faults, I see the system working well and don't believe one can have it both ways. Either you're all in, or you're out.

Expats and immigrants are two different animals. I am an immigrant. I'm all in. The system is set up on a sliding scale to take care of those who make a solid effort when they happen to be down on their luck. I feel France has been on my side every step of the way.

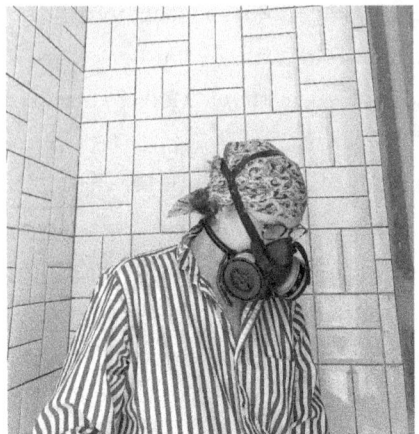

Terrell finishing a tile job while wearing one of my good shirts.

Restoring one hundred year old curved glass windows that overlook the Panthéon.

Not only did Madame set me up in style, later, my wife also experienced the same quality of service. In addition to her artist's visa, Terrell received a designation as a designer, which allowed her to work with me and receive Covid relief as well.

After my pilgrimage to *la Chambre du Commerce*, I was asked by a stunned spectator, "Do you know how hard it is to receive a designation?"

"No," I said.

When Madame finished punishing the keyboard, I was an *Auto Entrepreneur, Intérieur Menuisier*—a self-employed, interior carpenter. No more climbing tall ladders on the sides of buildings, being on roofs, in crawlspaces, or working in the rain. I was well on my way to having a social security number, *Siret* and *Siren* numbers and a *Carte Vital*, the French health card, not to mention a *Carte Européenne d'Assurance Maladie*, good anywhere in the European Union. What she did was put me on sound footing for all things that entail becoming French.

In Seattle I spent an inordinate amount of time cursing the speed demons and laggards while stuck behind the wheel of my truck. Here, I don't drive and focus my frustrations elsewhere. Bonus material, no car payment or broken side mirror repair costs, gas, insurance, parking garage or tickets. Now, I'm a low carbon footprint guy who line dries clothes—another positive negative. Barring strike days, not driving is only made possible by the world's most efficient public transit system and the city's electric bicycles. The fact that I don't have a valid French driver's license also plays a part. There are eighteen States that have reciprocity agreements with France, and Washington State is not one of them. So, what must a remodeling contractor, bent on chasing the almighty euro do? Become a construction sherpa.

Logistically, my learning curve has been steep. I've been forced to get familiar with the layout of the city and proximity of the home improvement stores in relation to each job site. Find the right style bag, that full of equipment, sits comfortably hanging off my shoulders. I carry a tile saw, table saw, shop vac, miter saw, mini-jack hammer, drills, levels, ladders, bags of hand tools, bags of bags, bags of hammers. Not all at once, that would be crazy, but piecemeal, everything I need to stave off starvation, and stay in the game.

Initially, I sweated where to dispose of all the construction debris. I found out the city sends trucks 'round to pick up most of it for free. The city government wants tourists on the streets, not garbage, hence the free pick-up—an aspect of socialism I hadn't considered. I distribute the weight I'm carrying to stay upright. It strengthens my sixty-five-year-old tendons, which allows me to keep power eating croissants as I march to my next gig. I get some strange looks but continue to soldier on and do what needs to be done to be self-supporting.

I recently had a hiccup on a jobsite. I fell flat on my back from up high on a ladder. There were tools and sharp objects all over the place and only enough space for me to land where I landed without cracking my head or worse. A sidewalk crime scene with a chalk outline where the dead guy used to be comes to mind. I landed smack inside the chalk lines. I thought my work life would be over, and it was, but only for five days. All I did was smash my gluteus maximus muscles and dislocate a finger, which I popped back into place. And instead of damaging myback, two bulged discs that had dogged me for twenty years course corrected on impact. The only reason I saw a doctor is because my wife hammered on me. My wife also hammers. A week later, I felt great. You won't find that remedy in any medical book.

Some buildings have no elevators, so I'm often forced to huff and puff my way six floors up the skinny spiral staircase. When some people move, the big items are delivered through the windows. A mammoth ladder with a platform extends up, off the up end of a truck parked on the street. It' a spectator sport. People gather to watch.

I've made a friend at *Plateforme du Batiment*, a wholesale supplier for contractors. I bought a compressor, which it turns out I didn't need, because walls here have no wood framing and brad nails don't shoot into plaster. A pneumatic nail gun came with the purchase, but they gave me two. After I returned the extra gun, Abu, my new friend, started showering me with free *Plateforme* T-shirts with the logo of every tool company imaginable. Bags of T-shirts. These have become parting gifts for all my friends who come to visit. Pseudo-Parisian contractors now roam the streets of Seattle.

While fixing a 250 year-old floor, I discovered a perfectly preserved rat skeleton, century unknown.

Chapter 13

Charming Mothers and Conjured Grandmas

Left to right, my mom, Virginia Monsarrat Piotter, brother Bill and aunt Donna Claire Monsarrat.

I received a Christmas card from my cousin Marcia, former drummer for the all-girl punk band The Klitz, in Memphis, Tennessee. Tucked inside the card, was a circa 1953 black and white glossy of two bathing beauties and a toddler. The card said, "Our charming mothers on the beach with

Billy boy. Pictures of uncles Buddy and Bobby to follow. Long live the Monsarrats." I never met my uncles, but I did read about one of them. In 2009, at eighty-six, a Red Tennessee Oak smashed through my Uncle Robert's roof, pinning him down with some bumps and bruises. It made the national news. He'd moved rooms just in time to catch Oprah. He claimed she saved his life. This would be his second fifteen minutes of fame. The first was when he helped liberate the Buchenwald death camp in WW II.

The beauties my cousin spoke of were my mom, Virginia, with her younger sister, aunt Donna Claire, and the toddler, my brother Bill, in the happier days two-or-so years before our secret family tragedy struck and claimed my mom's son, Richard. I'm not clear if I can call him my brother, since he died before I was born. My dad, Bill Sr. dropped their number two son, ten-month-old Richard, on his head, causing his death and accelerating the death of their marriage. Mine wasn't a family who voluntarily processed feelings through shared information. We *were* a family who—whatever was eating at us—sucked it up and suffered in silence. Interrogations didn't even help. Never in my lifetime did either of my parents acknowledge Richard's short life. At nineteen, I discovered Richard's existence by liberating his death certificate from a lock box while on the hunt for family secrets. Once I was in the know, my siblings invited me into the fold and provided some sketchy details.

The photo roiled in me like an emotional lava lamp. I believe that the death of Richard had a profound effect on the trajectory of my family. I'd love to blame this event as the sole catalyst for all my worldly woes, but somehow I became a willing participant. The Tennessee Monsarrats would heal just fine, they had the salve of a loving tight-knit family who *did* process feelings through shared information. By the time I arrived in 1960, a family camera was of a bygone era. There's just one photo of me as a child on Topsy the pony, a bucolic prop.

My Father went AWOL from the military and disappeared for a year to parts unknown, but was given a pass because of his service in WW II and Korea. During his time out my mother leaned on her family for support, financial and otherwise. After Bill Sr.—who I think of as *Ill Will*—sculked back to his dreaded obligations, the Navy sent him to the far-flung Kingdom of Hawaii, at the time not even part of the country.

In the ensuing years support from my dad waned. When he quit his job, support then dried up altogether. In '71 he decided he was done with his raising a family charade. His exit screamed loud and clear—there was nothing for him in Seattle. He didn't have to say he wasn't coming back, we knew and that was okay with us. He'd traded us in for the wilds of Alaska, to "have a go at running a business," which was code for hide, drink and sleep late. I was way ready to let *my* freak flag fly, which as an adult, led to me attempting escape from self by running away to Alaska.

Until 2017, I'd only ever met my Memphis family one time. In 1975, my dad had swooped back in to nurture a brainstorm. He kidnapped my sister Pam, me and my mom for an epic white trash road trip to impinge upon both sides of our estranged families. We flew to St. Louis and drove to Michigan. Then Michigan to Memphis and on to Florida, eating gas station food along the way. I wanted to ask why we didn't fly to Michigan then drive to Memphis but was afraid that being smarter than my dad would cost me.

We caught glimpses of and imposed upon every living relative we'd been avoiding up until then, turning into three-day old fish. I could see the bitterness spill from their eyes. When my sister Pam and I were introduced to my dad's dad, the most bitter of them all, he said, "Hmmm" then turned his back on us and walked away. *Nice to meet you, grandpa.* I never did get a chance to turn my back on him.

One of the things I remember most about being fifteen and on the road trip, was my dad liked to wave his gun around and make proclamations. If he got any serious lip from any of the locals, *Pow!,* he aimed to show them the business end. My feeling was he might shoot one of us. Being a weed sneak protected me from the very real dangers of being the son of Ill Will.

When my aunt Donna Claire came with my cousins to my house in Seattle in 2017, she told me she'd read my memoir, *Fixed*. She said, "If I'd have known how y'all lived, I'd have taken you in to live with me." I knew she meant it. She died three years later at ninety-three. My brother, Billy boy, was taken by AIDS in 1993, at age 44 and my mom ceded to lung cancer in 2011. On her death bed, she revealed many a family anecdote, but still, never acknowledged baby Richard.

Marcia has plans to visit Paris. We're both très keen on catching up. I find myself the only uncle of the children of my only sibling who chose to parent. After my niece had her first, she claimed, 'now, you're a great uncle." I thought, *that's weird, why just last week I was mediocre, at best.* I still don't quite know how all this family business works, but I figure what I do know I came by honestly.

CONJURING UP GRANDMAS

Parisians do their living outside, on display and unapologetically. I see the damnedest things here, like teenagers loving on their parents in public and vice versa. Here, family matters. I am awed. In sharp contrast, as a twelve-year-old it was clear to me that life as a Piotter would never evolve into a loving family unit. I knew my siblings loved me but with what transpired before my arrival, my parents' tools had long been dulled.

My brother Bill and sister Vicki got the memo early and made a break beyond the iron fist towards their respective glimmers of hope. My dad followed their lead, unaware that it was him they were escaping. That left me, the last out of the canal, my sister Pam and my mom to try and keep our own glimmers from going dark. We were a triangle of confusion seeking comfort any way we could get it. Pam did okay, but the message I received was, *get lost,* which with my imagination was not hard to do. By swaddling myself in weed and other vehicles, childhood was a time capsule I avoided all the way into adulthood.

I'd heard talk of grandmas and the like but had never set eyes on the fabled familial matriarchs. Extended family was seldom mentioned and if it was, only in vague terms. Pain and shame have a way of slamming doors. I'd groomed myself to be a self-starting, go-getter type and knew that the old folk's home up over the hill housed scads of perfectly good grandmas ready to receive grandsons. My friend Jeff was also a tribeless throwaway, so we teamed up to investigate what looked like a giant gingerbread house for a grandma safari. If successful, there'd be no doubt we could all find common ground in bagging on our *real* families. The grannies for being parked there, and us for being neglected.

Concerned over a potential grilling, I stated our purpose, "We're here to see our grandmas," to the gatekeeper.

"Go on then," we were told. We split up and peeked in rooms until we both found what we deemed suitable and inviting grandmothers. I told my newfound grandma I was a star little league baseball player, tops in Mrs. Volz sixth grade class and all the rest of the things I knew I wasn't. Things she probably knew were bald-faced lies, but let me keep my dignity anyway.

As fast as I talked, I'm sure she accurately sized me up for what I was, an unsupervised, confused child and headed for trouble. That I was a stranger to her was of no concern. On that day, she was my loving grandmother, benevolent through and through. I took her up on an invitation to return. So I did. Even though she'd been replaced by someone, it seemed like we kicked right back up where we'd left off. Over the course of the next few weeks Jeff and I collected a gaggle of grandmas who I imagined to be just as good as the real thing. I see intergenerational love on display in Paris, but wouldn't it be something if on a global scale, people treated each other the way our adopted grandmas treated us way back when?

Chapter 14
An Unforgettable Chapter

I've just passed the fifth anniversary of my urban drubbing when I almost lost my ear. It was seven o'clock on a bleak and frigid December morning. The Paris jackhammers were still quiet and the air was clean. I carried my computer bag, which housed a collection of dog-eared paperbacks, my preferred vehicle for check out during the cheek-to-jowl Metro rides. Reading is great for avoiding eye contact with the ever-present flock of scripted panhandlers. Before I hid behind paperbacks, I used to deviate from the plot line and stare at my fellow Parisian riders with my mouth agape, catching flies and writing stories about their lives. I pondered body mass index, what societal rung they were stuck on and who'd crushed their fingers while on the way up. What quack did their duck-lipped collagen injections and what part of their index the fat came from.

My shoulder bag is just a solid-black utilitarian affair from another generation and in Paris, it's almost a fashion affront. I often wonder why my attacker went after such an anonymous bag when there's so many to choose from. I'm not the only one with an imagination, I know what it's like to be driven by wishful thinking. I should have just carried the books in my hand.

Then, BLAMMO! Out from behind a fluted column, up popped a psychopath who deputized both of his two-pound fists to deliver me a coded message. Sometimes pain just can't be explained and suffering tags along for the ride. Metro construction had been ongoing for almost a year, and the sidewalks were cordoned off with metal panels, which created an inescapable kill-zone. I remember saying, "What the fuck dude" while wobbling like the Tin Man on my fizzling frame.

The frothing thirty-something packed a wallop. He hit me three or four times in the forehead before I could put two and two together and when I did it no longer equalled four. I had twenty-five years on him and he had twenty-five kilos on me. For him it was just another day at the office. He appeared to know what he was doing. Pre-brain damage, I could've stomped him in a debate.

Concerning places to take a beating, my shiny forehead proved the best place to receive. Me being hair challenged increased his available space for an easy target. He connected with no soft fleshy tissue, just a mass of knuckle bruising bone, extra thick to protect my priceless thought clouds that perpetually roll through. Futility appeared to make him madder. He continued with his fruitless endeavor. My two black eyes—blood and inflammatory fluid which migrated from my forehead—would be gravity induced. I would take on the appearance of a bandit.

The neanderthal came at me with another barrage. I thought of *The Fast Runner*, a first-date movie I for some reason agreed to see with Terrell after we'd just met. For entertainment, Eskimos punched each other in the head until there was no detectable brain activity. Fun for the whole family. I went out for boxing when I was ten, got punched in the nose within the first five seconds and that was it. I started smoking weed instead. That did the trick. I remember wondering, *What's this woman's angle?* I hated that movie.

Felled and on my way down, I caught my ear—spurt, spurt—on a jagged chunk of metal. That's when he put the boots to me. From my point of view, they could have used a shine. I did a somersault, popped back up and fought like an inflatable fabric stick figure. I've no doubt the guy intended to kill me. I *was* able to gift him one good one while I still had something in the tank—a tattoo of Nathan Hale, an imprint from my deceased brother Bill's class-ring—before I turned into Jell-O. *Gooo Raiders!* He was impressed. My only regret was, I didn't have another tattoo to give. He articulated some more indecipherable psycho-pathetic gobbledygook. I shudder to think what would have happened if he'd set his sights on a feeble person not so hard-headed as me.

There's a billboard in my old Seattle neighborhood that says stubbornness kills x number of men every year. X being a big number. As a younger man, I would've toughed it out to make my case, but I came to the reality that the portions he served up were larger than the portions that I could dish out and, going forward, I'd need teeth to eat. So, for dessert, I cut my losses and became a fast runner.

I was wearing my favorite Jackson Pollock scarf, and the blood seemed to mix in perfectly. A Good Samaritan, who I could no longer see, cyphered I was in a world of hurt and asked a redundant question, "Is everything okay?" then called the police, who in turn called that freebie ambulance. The grunting hellion darted across street but gave it up when a crowd gathered.

After my public beat-down, I called my wife from the hospital. "Don't panic," I said, "I'm at the hospital, I've been attacked." Panicked, she said, "Aaaaaaaaaa!"

"Stay inside, there's a maniac on the loose," I said. After she wailed like those sirens, she calmed down and went outside to retrieve my crazy expensive alpaca hat, which softened the blows. But my prized space-aged German eyeglasses did get lost in the melee. *Scheiße.*

Talk about a loser. Where were all those killer Bruce Lee maneuvers I practiced while watching movies and smoking weed as a kid? What'd I do with Spock's Vulcan nerve pinch? I certainly didn't have time to unpack his logic box on the guy. Or any of the other moves that lived at the forefront of my spring-loaded cerebral cortex, itching for a situation such as this. Shaky camera work aside, I'd seen Matt Damon's Jason Bourne character dispatch countless villains and had watched Liam Neeson kick everybody's ass in Hollywood. When I was a kid, I hacked my way through innumerable dirtbags during flights of fancy. It shouldn't have gone down the way it did. I should've been tougher. I had no idea that age and bone density would factor in.

The bad part about getting punked in public isn't the blows to the head, I can take those, been doing it all my life, it's all the glaring looks—some fear, some disgust—coming from total strangers. An odd assortment of jurists hung about the hospital lobby to pass judgement on me. *Just another despicable nobody who got what he deserved*, or so I perceived. Toxic laser beams like theirs are usually reserved for rape-Os on a perp walk. My mind was working overtime.

On the way out of the hospital—shortly after my dignity funeral—my iPhone also died. So, no more map. *"Excusez-moi, excusez-moi,* can you tell me where I live?" When Paris was built, the grid wasn't even a concept. I walked for what seemed miles down one back alley after another only to end where I'd started. Dumb luck finally intervened and I bumbled my way home. The incident had happened in front of a radiology clinic. You'd think they could have put one of those crazy-expensive cameras on the outside of the building, so we could have verified the guy was bigger and younger and had no heart. But no! Not a single surveillance camera to be found to verify my alibi for being such a weenie.

The next night at the police station—I was required to file a report if I wanted a little help paying for new glasses—the looks of disgust softened and had been replaced with pity. My face had gone green and appeared that at any moment it might die and fall off my head. Me, the ex-bank robber, ex-convict-criminal-reprobate, was there for once not as part of a line up, but as a rat to look at one.

A beefy female Sargent straining against her uniform spun the photo album around and pushed it across the table. "What did he look like?" she asked.

I flipped through and thought about it. *He had a bald muscled head carved out of a block of granite. He looked like life had dealt him some severe blows. He looked like me only heavier, younger, stronger, olive skin, with dark, suspicious basket-case-hardened-eye-sockets. A forehead so pronounced, one could stand under it and stay dry in a rainstorm, a real, knuckle-dragger. Like him, and him, and that one.* They all had that hard, pinched look of defiance, or they all needed to go to the bathroom.

I must admit I'd lumped the scrum together. They'd become the same guy—a thug cluster. Before I moved to Paris, I had a neighbor, a black dude, who walked two boxers—not pugilists, but dogs—and not at the same time. He had to walk them separately because they couldn't wait to get into the ring with each other. Then one died, followed shortly thereafter by the other. Boxers are notoriously susceptible to heart disease. This I found out from his wife, who on occasion, while walking my own dog, I chatted with about the sad state of our crime-riddled neighborhood and beyond. Later, when I saw him walking alone, I said to him, "Hey man, sorry about your boxers." He looked at me, puzzled, then looked down, to see if his fly was unzipped. Wrong guy, an honest mistake, but still.

I thought of this while flipping through perp pages. Having occupied squares in books like that myself, I didn't care to pin an assault on anyone, even *those* mugs. The episode had run its course, so poof, I let it go. Whoever he was, he had a heavy cross to carry and suffered every single day just living inside his skin. Four months later, in the thick of the Covid lock down, I looked out my window, there he was, obviously drunk and howling into space, while he pushed a baby buggy full of scavenged possessions. I felt sorry and wondered why I was spared from that degree of crazy. But not that sorry, but for the grace of God, better him than me.

The episode didn't sway my opinion that Paris is a safe and inviting city. I've seen no guns, other than law enforcement. In my old neighborhood of South Seattle, I happened upon spent cartridges all the time. The streets were littered with them. I lost a tenant from my mother-in-law apartment due to a fresh bullet hole in the neighbor's car. "Oh that, I wouldn't worry, that happens all the time." An awkward statement meant to reassure, but the best I could come up with on the spur of the moment. Then poof, she fled somewhere not so Glock happy.

My head healed up nicely. I went back to the hospital to get my stitches out. I was told, "We only put stitches in, we don't take them out. You must go to ..." (insert the voice of Charlie Brown's teacher, with a French accent). They gave me the address of a hospital across the town. There was yet another Metro strike which hobbled the city, so after visiting every bicycle kiosk, only to find bent frames, flat tires and broken foot pedals, I zombie walked myself across town. When I got where I was going, I was informed I needed to have a form filled out by my family doctor to have the stitches taken out. *Huh?*

I said, "I don't have a family doctor."

"Go get one and come back." I limped back home to my wife. After she watched a YouTube video on how to remove stiches, she swooped in with scissors and tweezers to finish me off. I let her know, "I'll be needing a cavity filled at some point." Good or bad, my head is still hard. If I had it to do all over again, I might have hit the streets wearing chainmail.

A NEW DECADE

February 22, 2020, was a day—unbeknownst to Jean Q. Publique—that the Covid virus was building up a full head of steam. There was also a celebration. My wife and I had started the practice of early morning Sunday bike rides around Paris—our training wheels and a precursor to daily commutes. That Sunday, we chose to noodle around Île-Saint-Louis. We had stayed on the island during our first visit and found it to be a tranquil and charming stand-alone village surrounded by the river Seine, in the middle of the city.

Notre Dame's copper coq, damaged but not dead, rests at Cité de l'architecture et du patrimoine. Its successor rests atop its new and rightful perch.

We wheeled our way into a procession of Zealots heading to the Catholic church on Rue Saint-Louis-en-l'Île. They had a gleaming copper rooster on display that was to be affixed to the top of the thirty-meter-high spire. This was less than a year after Notre Dame caught fire and the city was still smarting.

We followed the procession and watched while the riggers hoisted the *coq* by crane to affix it to its new home—the cap on a multi-year, multi-million-euro renovation project. Later, I was happy to learn that the procession was made up of sixty-seven shop keepers and a flock of priests, all doing business on l'Île.

Chapter 15

In the Tube

Paris is a compact city of two point one million people, shaped like an out-of-round cinnamon roll, or snail, if you like. And according to the topography of the sidewalks, lots of little dogs live here too. It's no more than seven miles across, at any given point. With a spider web of underground tunnels, the Metro system transports over four million passengers a day to anywhere in or around the city, in about forty minutes. Many books can be read while commuting, what's not to love? Except unmasked sneezers, so mask up.

When you come, brace yourself for the non-violent but dependably annoying pickpocket contingency. On the tourist heavy lines, there's a never-ending public service announcement in multiple languages every ten minutes alerting passengers to the fact. There's even an American jazz singer posted up belting out a warning about them. Pickpockets usually work in threes—one male and two females. The guy takes a picture of the potential target's low hanging fruit and texts it to his female counterparts, then they home in. One trips and falls into the ignorant arms of their victim while the other two converge, clog and confuse. A sprinkling of drawn-out sweet talk throws enough shade for her two counterparts to make the pinch and hand-off the goods to Mr. iPhone. Then presto, all three turn into ghosts. Rinse and repeat.

Me and a few of the other 4 million people a day who travel underground in Paris.

As a greenhorn Parisian, I got lucky. I was spared. A pickpocket, also green, clumsily accosted my back pocket with designs on my exposed iPhone. I clamped his soon to be bloodless wrist until he let go of the phone, apologetically morphed into a shrug emoticon and spun off into the scrum. Without government assistance, Covid-19 made it tough for pickpockets. Now they're back and more determined than ever to prosper at tourists' expense.

I love the efficiency with which the electric Metro system moves the masses. Because I no longer drive, people are no longer idiots. Not contributing to the dirty death of the planet is a breath of fresh air and I'm happy about that too. But on the Metro not everyone is in a state of bliss.

Almost as soon my wife and I arrived and descended into the belly of the beast, we were slapped with the tangy fusion of piss and perfume—a precursor to the forthcoming oddities that I'd be slapped with, like the young, volatile woman who exposed and weaponized one of her breasts. She shoved it in my face and asked, "What are you looking at?"

Rendered speechless, I scrunched my face up and blinked, then turned red and thought, *man, if you don't know, I can't explain it to you,* but said, "Abadē-abadē-abadē" instead. A few blinks later, she'd marched on in search of an answer. I really hope she didn't forget her baby on one of the Metro cars.

Some Metro cars are newer than others, with double-layered safety doors. One go-getter got his foot stuck in both doors at waist level when the doors closed. Spring-loaded and ready to serve, my wife catapulted herself towards the emergency stop lever while an anonymous French guy and I scrambled to pry the doors open. We accessed enough internal boy scout juice to allow him to pull his foot back in and say goodbye to a shoe. A shoe I'd previously walked a mile in. A shoe he should have given the boot long before. The train finally screeched to a halt and the doors abruptly opened. The agitated driver hustled over to interrogate the frenzied foot soldier. There must have been a logical explanation.

Eighteen years ago, a woman high-sided an ambulance on a ten-inch concrete curb which ran parallel to the rockery in front of my house. The rig threatened to teeter over the embankment, so I sprinted to my garage and came back with a thick plank and a short log to create a fulcrum. I wanted her to be on her way and continue to collect damaged goods to fill the hospitals with. I'd almost MacGyvered her to safety when a suspicious, crime-fighting neighbor tackled and pinned her down in preparation for her mugshot.

Seems she'd happened upon an idling, narcotics-filled ambulance and took it for a joy ride. This to say, as a useful idiot, I sometimes miss the beat. I had no idea what was going on with the shoeless rider man. A heated discussion ensued between the driver and one shoe. It sounded *très cool*. While four arms flailed and two beaks bumped. I asked a bi-lingual biped, "What's *that* all about?"

He told me, "The driver asked him, "What the hell are you doing?" Then said, "This is the third time today you've done this!" It appears to be his hustle." A hard way to make a euro, since France is void of ambulance chasers and not a litigious society. But I get it, shoes or no shoes, somehow a guy's got to get through the day.

But, it's not all fun and games underground. Of the fourteen Metro lines, three are automated—no driver. The oft overlooked reality that driver bot doesn't care about your wellbeing can ruin the vacation of the euphoric, clueless tourist. There are signs posted aplenty, in easy-to-understand cartoon instructions. Rabbits with broken legs and bandaged heads, long tongues hanging sideways and x's where eyes should be. Yet, disaster continues to strike.

While riding Line 1 at Place de la Concorde, I watched a young woman blow off the blaring buzzer and leap full of glee and haute couture to try and make the cut. Time, tide and automation waits for no one. Two doors closed on her arm. The first door was part of the train and took off, capable of taking an arm along for the ride. The second door—part of the platform—pinched her arm at the shoulder, also threatening amputation. She was lucky to be travelling with a companion who, after shitting in his pants, thought fast, grabbed her around the waist and ripped her loose. Her handbag and just purchased high fashion items were stripped away, ground into sludge under the train's greasy wheels. As a parting gift, she got to keep her lavender blue arm and the notion she got off easy.

I too had a bad experience underground. I was confronted by a female Metro cop who bandied about her status like *un coq*. She strutted purposefully towards my wallet over a spent Metro ticket that I'd discarded. Seems riders are supposed to hang on to them to prove they've not jumped the turnstile. Those rules are also posted. At the time, my lack of language skills deemed me *Ignoramus Americanus*.

I'd been in the habit of tossing my spent ticket as soon as I got through the turnstile. To recoup lost revenue from the bazillions of annual thriftsters, Métro Police periodically set up sting operations. According to my wife, the female rooster said, "No ticket, ninety Euros." A ninety euro fine for not having a spent ticket would sting plenty. Her French became as clear as my indignation, while my English devolved. To me, this qualified as a government shakedown. I puffed out my own chest and said, "I ain't payin' no ninety euros."

Bent on ruining my day, she continued badgering my personal translator for information. *"What did he say?"* I was ready to go the distance, based on principal. I had put my wife in a pinch by expecting her to lie for me.

"He says he's very sorry he threw away his used ticket and respectfully asks your forgiveness."

Their back-and-forth was interspersed with me popping off indecipherable mumblings. I must have swatted down a kilo of tunnel flies with my gesticulating. She came to understand that the punishment I'd get from my wife going forward would be at least ninety euros worth and settled for watching me tear up a valid ticket and sent us on our way. My wife had gone to bat for me. Another vaporous victory before a blanket of silent scorn wrapped me up and sent me to bed early. But hey, I went to bed early in Paris.

Paris is a melting pot. It's not uncommon to see drag queens in all shapes, sizes and nationalities. Drag queens are tough, so if a contestant chooses to slap a drag queen with a white glove, they'd better be up for the duel or have a good second advocating for reconciliation without violence.

One fixture in my first Paris neighborhood was a person who, from a mug shot's point of view, looked like a Hell's Angel or Russell Brand. But when viewed from behind, multiple valid questions could be raised. This neck-up-biker wore a mink, sported a mini-skirt, fishnets, stiletto heels and stoked plenty of confusion in his wake. On cobblestone streets that's quite the investment. Not even in the Olympics have I seen a more developed pair of calf muscles. With fists balled up like two beating hearts and shoulders hunched, Queenie tramped around with purpose, and didn't appear to be open to debate.

When a group of testosterone handicapped teenagers sat down next to another formidable queen on the Metro, the ringleader may not have realized Queenie stood about 6'5" and was seriously muscled up. One minute the young buck was holding court, yuckin' it up with his entourage at Queenie's expense. The next, he'd been lifted off his seat by long fingers with high gloss nails. He would get no intervention from his born-again, peace-loving cohorts.

I didn't stay for the punch line. I jumped off, then back on the next car. I'm sure there was a valuable lesson learned. I'm happy to report that Parisians live and let live. The antagonists are few and far between, and the fabric of society finds a way to get along.

Pre-Covid, us oldsters could always count on the French youth to snap to and rapturously vacate a seat to let us take a load off. Not anymore. Now it's, "You fucked up our planet, you can just stand there and think about what you've done. Now if you'll excuse me, I have some soup to throw at the Mona Lisa." That's some attitude. I can't say that I blame them.

One of the sounds emanating from the tube in Paris, besides, *"Where the fuck is my wallet?"* is the sound of the buskers. These fixtures are on the world's list of oldest professions. Once you get a listen—as with the oldest profession—you'll be hooked. RATP, the French state-owned enterprise that operates public transportation in Paris, only awards three hundred permits, which require renewal twice a year, to over two thousand applicants. You'll find the seventeen hundred musicians not chosen car jumping on the Metro, practicing for their next shot at *the Bigs*. Competition is fierce and the bar is high. I heard a world-class string ensemble playing Rimsky Korsakov's *Flight of the Bumble Bee*. I became so distraught by the frenetic arrangement that I boarded the wrong train.

At another Metro stop, a solo artist wailed on a shofar, a.k.a. God's alarm clock. It said, *Wake up heathens and give me some money.* For the uninformed, this lonely instrument is typically played on Yom Kipur, a day of fasting and atonement. The guy did appear to have missed a few meals but he was out there wailing day and night. I'm not sure if that moved him closer to or further away from God. What he lacked in tone, he more than made up for in stick-to-it-iveness, and there was certainly nothing wrong with his lungs. A lot could happen until the next tryouts. With some serious practice and divine intervention, he just might make the leap.

An Aaron Neville doppelganger sang into his hoagie sandwich microphone, paused for a snack attack and hummed the outro *Everybody Plays the Fool* with his mouth full. Next stop, a young Bowie clone displayed his badge for the RATP workers and expertly took me on a flight to Mars. On the connecting platform, a deaf elderly Chinese man—who had a good stretch of it for himself—played the ancient erhu at Spinal Tap levels, while the grimacing crowd huddled on the opposing end. The acoustics are amazing in the tube. There seems to be a Romanian school of gypsy jazz, many have the same set list.

One maestro plays intricate, American jazz standards on a cheap, plastic melodeon keyboard flute. He sings like Louis Prima. He's so talented he always manages to transform the collective mood in the Metro cars. One car after another, to the end of the line, then back the other way. I always dig for a little something extra and hope that his cup will forever runneth over. Buskers work hard for their money and that I can respect.

Chapter 16
Epic Paris Apartment Hunt

After our landlady rolled the dice and leased my wife and me her Paris apartment, there's a chance I became a touch too smug with our good fortune. I didn't have the hindsight to appreciate all the flaming hoops I'd soon be jumping through for a few hundred square feet, while masked up trying to stay one step ahead of the killer Corona virus. I was still unfamiliar with the weight and magnitude of the rental dossier—the monolithic stack of paperwork which looms large over even the most well-healed Parisian's head. It's easier to buy a house in the States than rent an apartment in Paris. I've since changed my tune. I may have been lucky, but I wasn't exempt.

Beware when renting long term from an Airbnb host, you might be pinched for space. After our first year, she asked us if we'd like to renew the lease. We said yes, with a paraphrased caveat: "Move all your bric-a-brac out, so we can claim a crumb of space for ourselves." She said, "Okay," which meant that *I* was to purchase large packing crates, box up all her bottom of the barrel furnishings and put them in the basement, which smelled like piss because the building's main plumbing waste pipe had holes in it and drip, drip, dripped right in front of our apartment's storage unit door. The chain of events hung heavy in the air.

A little backstory on the shifting winds emanating from our landlord. What was once a gentle breeze, encouraging us to move along at our leisure, had become a hurricane-force certified letter threatening legal action. Prior, a water spot had developed on our ceiling, an occurrence that strikes fear into the heart of every Parisian who owns an apartment. In Paris, plumbers get the bow and scrape treatment. Logic and gravity told me that an apartment above was responsible for the damage. *Au contraire.*

Our renter's insurance policy indicated *we* must pay and then some time down the road, might get reimbursed if they couldn't find a way to pin the blame on us. I felt a pang, but as a guest in France, knew I should zip it and bend over to take my medicine. We have since learned that if the apartment is rented furnished, the landlord is on the hook for repairs. A detail neither our landlord or the insurance company made known to us. *Where's the Complaint Department?*

We were required to vacate for ten days while repairs took place but had nowhere to go. I would have been happy to fix it, but she had already made a deal with someone else. She and her husband bit the bullet and invited us to stay at her family estate one hundred miles to the south, while he and she were out of town. All we had to do was take care of the cat. Who can't take care of a cat?

Our forced retreat took place during a summer *canicule* (heat wave) which reached one hundred seven degrees. Seems when we shuttered the place up and headed for the train station back to Paris, we'd inadvertently trapped the curious feline in one of the outbuildings without access to water. *Oopsie.*

Apparently, it used up a hand full of lives but survived and lived to get trapped another day. I made the mistake of mentioning to our landlord my displeasure that the reimbursement for the ceiling repair only came in at seventy-five percent. It pushed me over the very real, complaining American cat-killer line.

Then there's the language. When writing in French, the nuances can sometimes spin out of control. One misplaced letter can turn a relationship upside down. For example, *vous-voulez des boissons?* is how to ask someone who you are *not* intimate with, if they would like *drinks*. But *vous-voulez baiser*, is how to ask someone you are *not* intimate with if they want to *fuck*, which could be interpreted as a bit too forward. And, if you ask someone if they're excited about something, you might as well say, "Are you orgasmic?"

When courting relationships, spell check is your friend. What was said in our return email wasn't quite as egregious as a sexual proposition, but Madame interpreted it as us saying, "Go fuck yourself and good luck trying to get us out." In her mind, we were the sons of Hibachi. A linguistic blunder, combined with a near cataclysmic feline death experience turned her against us. Hence, the registered, *get, the f...k out of my apartment*, letter. In two short years divorce was imminent, the honeymoon over.

To gloss over the discomfort of being ejected while Covid raged, she said, "My granddaughter needs a place to live while she attends art school." As if that would've given us comfort. At the time, nobody was going to school in person, so I knew *that* was bunkum.

Three months before our GTFO mandate, we got down to the business of looking for apartments on Orpi, Seloger, PAP, Leboncoin, and the rest of the housing websites. We took notes on desired amenities and what we couldn't live without: bathtub, balcony, American-style kitchen, hardwood floors, millwork and built-ins. Everything our twenty-five-hundred square foot house in Seattle had, except a yard.

After lopping off chunk after chunk of must-haves, we climbed back down to the hardscrabble, deciding we couldn't live without an apartment. Out of our mammoth ledger of potential habitats, we barely got a call back. When we did, one friend said, "A call back, that's amazing." In Paris, unfurnished doesn't just mean no furniture, it can include the absence of a stove, fridge, sink, cabinets, countertops or lighting, as was the case with one "furnished" apartment we looked at. The proprietor waved her arm across expanse of the gutted kitchen and said, "Look, we've remodeled!"

Once we got a glimpse of the squalid stock available, we knew caulk salesmen were doing a bang-up business. I must give props to the ultra-talented real-estate photographers, there are some *real* clunker apartments out there. Pandemic or not, the day we had to be out of the three hundred and fifty square foot apartment was bearing down on us like old age. Nonetheless, I clung to the thought, *with our maturity and the forty-page dossier Terrell had put together, we were sure to be shoo-ins.*

I'm well familiar with the feeling of not being picked for say, dodge ball, sex, or early release from prison. Competition for square meters in Paris is fierce. There was always someone with more money, younger and better looking who farted less. We called over two hundred and fifty places and looked at twenty-five. I clung to the fanciful list of our dream apartment's desired amenities and taped it to the wall. We just couldn't bring ourselves to sign up for the pigeonholes on offer.

France is relational, so I never pass on the opportunity to hear my lovely voice squawk about my challenge du jour to anyone within earshot. Out of nowhere, a British expat I'd met and swapped numbers with, called. Straight from my index of maladjustments, I thought that because of her Queen's English, she was stuck up and didn't like me and would never call.

She said, "My daughter has a friend who just bought a place ten days ago, then immediately got transferred to the U.K. for work. She's painting the place now to get it ready to rent. You should go see it." The apartment, in the heart of Montmartre, came with a bathtub, hardwood floors, American style kitchen with new appliances, a washing machine, floor to ceiling windows and a view of Sacré-Coeur.

I was *très* keen on a washing machine. For two years, rain or shine I schlepped our dirty laundry up hill to the laundromat, a haven for early morning inebriants in need of warmth and a free change of clothes—the washers lock, but the dryers do not. The apartment appeared palatial compared to the one we were being eighty-sixed from. Albeit every inch was painted blood red. It had jumped off the page of my wish list.

The owner said, "I have a friend who wants it."

We said, "We'll help you paint, if you rent to us." That sealed the deal. Over the next three days—after securing the perfect apartment—we turned red into white and no longer felt so blue. Dossier, schmossier, neener neener neener.

I can be a bit of a klutz. I've been known to break things, though not on purpose. So I do accept responsibility for the breakage, with a disclaimer. In the apartment we were leaving, the plates were bigger than the sink and every time I tried to flip one over to rinse, I'd whack a hunk off with an assist from the absurdly low sink faucet. Porcelain is supposed to be tough, but it's as though they were Hollywood props made from sugar. The kitchen was so small that a cutting board straddling the sink was our only counter space.

Who leaves 1920's gold-rimmed Limoges dishes in a rental with plastic folding chairs? First, we ate off the dinner plates, until they were gone—which made me feel bad—then we ate off two salad plates each, which tricked me in to thinking I ate less, which felt good. After reducing the complete wedding set to a bag of driveway fill, I scoured the city looking for vintage Limoges without success. I couldn't find any wormholes to go back in time and get the originals, so we bought knockoffs at Le Bon Marché. Double ouch!! I wasn't allowed to even look at them until the key handoff.

When we did have the final walkthrough to check for damages, I sucked it up and came clean about the dishes. "Sorry about the bag of rubble." I was afraid she'd be unhappy with the replacements I'd chosen at Le Bon Marché, the namesake my mother worked at in Seattle, during the holidays, to keep the heat on and my dad in booze, when I was a kid. We called it, *The* Bon Marché.

She said, "Those are nice."

On my way back from the world's largest flea market at Saint-Ouen during Covid with the first piece of furniture for our new apartment. Goodbye plastic bucket.

Monsieur said, "Dishes break, that's what they do." He gave me a commiserating wink. Madame gave him a look of admonishment. We received a full refund on the damage deposit. I now have my own dishes to plow through.

Shortly after we moved to our new apartment in Montmartre, our old landlord called to say, "Good news, my granddaughter won't be moving in after all. You can re-rent my apartment if you like." We thought, *That's a good one. Tell us another.*

Chapter 17
I Get Around

What a gift it is to not be stuck behind the wheel of a car or turning a wrench under one. I haven't contributed to Big Oil for over seven years. It feels good not being a hostage to fossil fuel. That's not to say I don't get around. I'm either underground ripping through books while shlepping my tools to the next job site, or above ground taking in the sights by bike or by foot. Any way I slice it, I'm a winner. Parisians aren't slender by chance.

As a newly minted Parisian, I want to share this good news with anyone who'll listen. But why should you believe me or any other convert trying to entice you to join the *grande fête*? Come see for yourself. Indulge in some French cuisine and a biting cup of coffee. Paris is a compact city, pulsating with possibilities. Here's some of what one can expect to see if one's willing to pull one's head out of one's smart phone.

East, along the Seine, starting at Bastille, is home to the prison that in the eighteenth-century housed many future headless heads of State. Over to Église Saint-Paul, a Baroque-style church birthed in 1647. Here considered slightly meh, but anywhere else, *magnifique*. Place des Vosges, just a cannon shot away, is considered the first European square. It was home to Victor Hugo who penned *Les Misérables* and *The Hunchback of Notre Dame*. Let's not get all weepy being caught up in historic literature. Time to move along or we'll get trampled.

The final phase of Notre Dame's exterior work before the scaffolding comes down.

The Centre Pompidou, conveniently located in the heart of Paris, spoke directly to me. I was drawn to the color-coded dystopian tubular structure, with all its plumbing, wiring, heat, refrigeration and climate control on the outside of the building. Its outsides look like the insides of the old U.S. Navy ships my father worked on and shlepped me to when I was a child. But the comparison ends there.

The savvy Pompidou Architects understood there's more room on the outside than on the inside, and the hell with what anyone thought. For Paris puritans stuck in the architectural Haussmann zone, dystopian took some getting used to.

The million plus square feet of floor space houses Europe's preeminent modern art collection, the rooftop restaurant Brasserie Georges, with its panoramic view of the city and a ground floor cafeteria. There's also the Acoustic Museum and Paris's first free public library, Centre Pompidou Bibliothèque, which I immediately homed in on.

Endless study tables accommodate all the young, future French policy wonks clacking away at their computers while envisioning clear-cut forests off to the pulp mills, to produce the stacks necessary to drive the socialist agenda.

As with any big city public library, a certain element is also encouraged to stimulate brain activity. When open, *Beware of Thief* warnings blare over the P.A. system at timed intervals. Apparently, the Centre Pompidou is a great place to duck out of the rain, take a load off, watch porn and snag some unattended computers. Or for those on the fringe, look up secret government websites that identify where the alien encampments are, watch porn and steal computers. All acceptable in the eyes of the library sheriffs. But red line, there will be no noise and no eating inside the library.

At the Centre Pompidou Bibliothèque, the circus is always in town. The collegiate study hall psych ward combo makes for total inspiration. Prior to joining the ranks of the semi-employed, I'd schlep my laptop across town to quietly produce pages for my yet to be realized life as a recognized literary stalwart.

Smell and behold. Enter Cheese Man, flagrant and foul and holier than thou. He reached inside his jacket layers and produced a respectable cheese platter, heavy on the bleu, then shot me a look which conveyed, *Rules are meant to be flaunted.*

Same time next day, again with the funkmeister fuller smorgasbord and the steely stare-down. I wiggled an eyebrow, which softened his mood. The French are tolerant live and let live types. No one seemed to be scandalized as he unwrapped his sampler and poured over Le Monde, rejuvenated and ready to brave the outside world.

Thanks for hanging. Now, it's back on the street and over to the Paris City Hall, an architectural marvel known as Hôtel de Ville. Be sure to keep that H silent. The south wing was built between 1535 and 1551 and the north wing, 1605 to 1628. One would never know that in 1871, it suffered a major fire started by the Paris Commune, a government that seized power and controlled swaths of the city during the Franco-Prussian war. Since the original plans were kept safe, the exterior was rebuilt exactly as it was, with the interior just slightly modified to the standards of the day. *Pas mal.*

Wherever I walk, I deftly practice my Fred Astaire moves to avoid the ornamentation laid down by man's best friend. Lawns are a rare commodity in Paris. *Et voila!* Like magic, it's all washed away by morning.

Across the street is BHV, the *everything* store where you'll never be able to spend enough money. I love BHV, except the accounts department, who I think of as, *The Knobs*.

I was recently tasked with the purchase of a complete set of extortionate hardware for sixteen interior doors—the final leg of what had been a very plumb gig. The thirty-eight hundred square foot apartment belongs to a Swedish couple who lives in Stockholm but likes to spend time in Paris at their pied-à-terre. Taking up the whole third floor of a building, it sits elevated, looking directly out onto the Panthéon in the 5th arrondissement—a neighborhood built by the Romans and the oldest quartier in the city. For over a year, I had the keys to another world. Imagining what it would be like to be fully flush with three working toilets.

BHV was a short walk to the job site, so they certainly received their cut. The door hardware bins were near empty, so I placed a partial order at the desk to keep the wheels of commerce spinning.

I was told, "We don't know when your order will arrive, but you can pick it up off the shelf when it does. That will be 528 €." I said, *'Ce n'est pas bon pour moi.* (That doesn't work for me). I'll pay when I pick it up, 'Merica,' which didn't work for them. We were *not* harmonious, so I canceled the order and bought it of the shelf, piece meal, over time, to the tune of 2700 €.

Later, the flood of threatening phone calls started to roll in saying I owed 528 € for the hardware I ordered. I scanned my door hardware receipts as proof of purchase and sent them via email up to the fifth-floor accounting department, where the punishing number crunchers plotted. For the next few months, I heard *diddly-squat*. Then, the counterfactual accountants were back, with renewed indignation. So, I gathered up my receipts and headed towards the battlefield.

I approached one of The Knobs and spit French gibberish at her while wildly flailing my arms. I've been known to be excitable. I thought, *someone needs to get down and kiss my ring*. Madame clerk got the gist of what I'd told her and pounced on the phone, wildly flailing her own arms, while giving the business in rapid-fire French to the person on the other end, who I imagine, punted the fresh indignities to an underling, until the lowest BHV minion kicked a dog, or sucker punched a Parisian cockroach.

Out of the shadows, a four-pack of misfiring employees converged upon me like store security. An experience I'm all too familiar with, but in that instance I didn't feel the need to fret. With leaky pen, the head honcho scratched out her email address on a scrap of paper and demanded I resend my stack of suspect receipts, despite me clutching them in my pulsating fists and the minor detail that I'd sent them before. Her longhand scribble-scratch resembled little the alphabet I grew up with. I had to hire a French code breaker to fulfill her request. Once decoded and sent, I waited for another response, which came weeks later from yet another accounting soldier not apprised of anything. Their team seemed to change with the seasons.

My friend Bruno, the French TV war correspondent, offered to go down with his camera and get a statement. He'd faced down enemies tougher than them and didn't feel they could significantly threaten him. He let me in on some effective legal mumbo-jumbo, sure to taint the top brass, leave a bad taste and create a buzz. I heeded his advice and let fly the tangy phrasing. Next came another round of silence. No apology. No gift card. No stock options. On the glass half full side, no emails and no more bullying phone calls. But I do love that store.

Back on course, it's onto Les Halles, which for centuries was a giant outdoor public market in the medieval sector. Much of the quartier was torn down over sanitary concerns and replaced with some of the forty thousand new-fangled nineteenth century Haussmann buildings. You can no longer buy live goats there, but you may find one dead on a spit and ready for the lunch crowd in the Marais.

As large as Emperor Napoleon made himself out to be, there are few monuments of him left in Paris. In Place Vendôme, the former warmonger shamelessly stands atop a 40-meter-high bronze column. He was a graduate of École Militaire in the 1790's, number 48 out of the 56 in his class. Mediocrity ruled. A dozen or so years later, he was coronated as Supreme Leader of France in Notre Dame cathedral. Man, did he know how to bring home other people's bacon. Before he became the big kahuna, he was affectionately referred to by his men as the Little Corporal.

Here's one of his quotes: "Glory is fleeting, but obscurity is forever."

Continuing west on the Rive Droite of the Seine, is the Louvre—just the most famous museum in the world—and a can't miss. On the other side—Rive Gauche—is the Musée d'Orsay, a former train station and home to the impressionists and pointillists, including Vincent Van Gogh and George Seurat.

Horsing around with my favorite effigy in the Richelieu wing of the Louvre.

If you're worn out from visiting the old masters at the Louvre, Renoir's smooshed fish-faced women at the d'Orsay, or the indecipherable modern art of the Pompidou, you can always go rogue and visit the bowels of Paris in the lesser known, less populated Paris Museum of Sewers. I shit you not.

You might come eye to eye with a giant rat mural or the occasional live one, but don't fret, you won't be confronted by Mr. Floatie, who's safely contained. Above ground or below, the smell is part of the package. The sewer has close to seventeen hundred miles of tunnels underground with street signs corresponding to the streets above so you don't get lost. There's even wi-fi, pronounced *wee-fee*, in case you can't take it and feel the need to check out. The museum is equipped with sound showers to remind you what it sounds like to get clean. If by chance, the sudden urge to evacuate does occur, there's a public toilet that—for your information—tracks the route of your offering. *Mais désolé*, if you get hungry, you'll be shit-out-of-luck. There are no restaurants down there just yet, so don't hold your breath for that reason.

Walk through le Jardin des Tuileries and onto Place de la Concorde and you'll set your eyes upon the 23-meter-tall Luxor Obelisk. In November 1830, Muhammad Ali Pasha, ruler of Ottoman Egypt, officially gave a pair of Luxor Obelisks to France—something Napoleon couldn't steal, although he did have designs on them. In return, France gave Egypt a clock that has since rarely worked.

It took seven years to get the Luxor Obelisk shipped, upright and on its pedestal in Place de la Concorde. A special boat was built for transport. François Mitterrand gifted the second obelisk—which never made it to France—back to Egypt. On December 1, 1993, demonstrators from Act Up Paris, an organization dedicated to fighting AIDS, covered the obelisk with a giant pink condom.

Continue west along the river and you'll see the le Grand Palais—built for the World Expo in 1889—and le Petit Palais, which is not so petit and has an amazing art collection of its own, free for the viewing. I'll be ice skating in the Grand Palais this Christmas season. Keep going and you'll be awed by La tour Eiffel, Gustave's famous erector set which structural engineers claim is ready to fall apart. *Hope the fresh paint holds it together.*

If you're willing to spend another forty-five minutes and burn off that last croissant, you can walk down the Champs-Élysées—a cobblestone boulevard, deemed the most beautiful in the world—and on to the Arc de Triomphe. If you're ultra-jazzed, keep going and eventually, you'll hit Deauville on the Atlantic. From there you'll have to swim. All that is just a fraction of what's on display. And north to south is nothing to sneeze at either.

While trekking across the city, something to keep in mind is that Parisian pedestrians move at warp speed. The only people I can liken them to are the stampede of psych-med recipients jockeying for pill line position when the call, *"Come and get it,"* blared over the prison loudspeakers. But unlike the prison gang, Parisians are not tooth challenged and neither are they dribbling spittle or dipped in ink. The point is, get in the flow or get out of the way. If one happens to be sightseeing, see faster.

My theory is it's a mad dash to park at an outdoor café to sip thimbles full of rancid coffee, burn never-ending Gauloises (which smell like mattress fires) and wax philosophically. Once they get where they're going, they do take their leisure time seriously. French daily planners are grayed out from 12:30 to 2:00 pm. They consider it criminal to work more than thirty-five hours a week. Little kids don't go to school on Wednesdays and have a holiday every six weeks. Then there is August, when the bowels of the city are emptied out. The city's inhabitants dump themselves in the countryside for the entire month. Many start their holiday as early as mid-July and don't return until the second week of September. I do wonder how anything gets done. Still, I'm starting to consider the merits.

I was out for a leisurely stroll, gawking at the architectural marvels when I heard, *"Allez-y, vieil homme."* My French is limited, but I knew she said, "Get it in gear, old man." Annoyance translates in any language. As a spreader of American sunshine, I responded, "It's a wide enough sidewalk, no need to crawl up my arse," so she'd think I was a Brit. Wouldn't want to give Americans a bad name, "And you don't appear to be so young, yourself."

I felt much better until she said, "I heard that" in English. I've since learned Paris is not like America, where you have personal space until someone robs or shoots you. Here, in the most condensed city in Europe, things are tight. That week, I got my heel stepped on multiple times and found myself with one shoe. The other shoe became a hockey puck on the Metro platform. I've since studied the Matrix and learned how to move like cyber-criminal Neo.

Vuitton's temporary construction façade on the Champs Élysée.

The Champs-Élysées is worth a second look. It's where the world's criminally wealthy stampede the boulevard to shop, shop, shop the stores into submission. And where mere mortals marvel at the madness. A daily reminder of the pampered life I'll never live. Uggs for Pugs and auxiliary furs for well-heeled dogs, but nary a plastic bag to scoop the gilded poop. Bling seekers continue to chase their dreams. Right now, the Louis Vuitton flagship store's façade is covered with a seven-story silver steamer trunk during construction, because the French cannot accept a less than visually stunning job site. It's a testament as to why the bags are so expensive.

You won't see any kids throwing tantrums for pastries on the Champs-Élysées. I gawked at twin babies being pushed in a double-wide stroller. Both pimped Ray-Bans and parted the sea of shoppers while lost inside their gold case iPhones. Walking on the Champs-Élysées is like visiting another museum filled with tourists. Bling-O-rama. Whole families and their entourages draped in the most expensive everything. *Pour moi*, it's a foreign land.

While out and about and at the mercy of my bladder, I was forced to bolt down a side street in search of a public toilet. Praise be to the bladder gods, who strategically scattered outhouse monstrosities on the sidewalks for the desperate and unpredictable, like me. It was a blip in time when a tech-savvy bathroom attendant would have come in handy. But virtual would have to do. Sensing my urgency, the door opened—*an invitation to step inside.* The door closed, opened and closed again, a comical malfunction in progress. An AI Molière.

I danced and stabbed at buttons while a French Siri enticed me with evocative commands from her hidden chamber. Siri seemed to enjoy toying with me. Just as I was able to coax action and get into the stream of life, my security status got flushed. The door opened and the toilet folded up inside the wall like a Murphy bed, exposing me to the critique of the queue. I was forced to wrap it up and dash off unsatisfied. No third option available. Travelers beware. For a good time, don't forget to download the Toilets of Paris App.

Chapter 18
Where Have I Been?

I've now surpassed the thirtieth anniversary of my full-ride scholarship into prison. It was my second free ride. Thanks for the third chance, taxpayers. It's hard to erase the ugly, embarrassing pre-prison memories of active addiction. How, while geeked out of my fricking mind from the steady stream of intravenous narcotics, government posse walkie-talkies squelched ever closer with the G-men ready to pounce, until the surge waned. How substances drove my agenda and paranoia kept me in hiding once I got where I thought I needed to be.

Illegal dumping was all the rage. When it came time to discard their junk, eco-cheaters were forever on the lookout for an out of the way, cost-saving patch of land as an alternative to the costly King County dump. North Acre's Park was billed as a family friendly greenspace but got encroached upon by the likes of me. It was within striking distance of the county dump and for many a last stop before ponying up.

I harken back to Tweaker's Academy, where dope fiends learn how to meticulously take things like televisions and stereos apart but never put them back together. I've since cleaned up and learned how to put things back together, like my life. Beyond the dreams that teased my reality, the deep dive into my sub-human ecosystem was always just one hit away.

Once the dose had run its course through my veins and venules, heart and gray matter, and exploded out through my sweat glands, my nervous system and my already dirty laundry, I calmed down enough to get a grip and shift my fragmented focus to a little frenzied treasure hunt. One man's garbage is another man's treasure. *Time to go to work. There's got to be something worth something around here somewhere.* It was the thought that perpetually fed my beast.

I figured I might as well make the best of being steeped in shit. Flies seemed to do all right by it. My hopes were also high as to what I might find. To my chagrin, all I found in that pile of illegally dumped junk was junk, and a lost colony of microbes. My scorecard read zero. The inhabitants clung to me like I clung to other people's stuff. As a needy codependent I had nothing to offer them in return.

It was a sweltering summer day, and my heart thumped out odd Afro-Cuban style rhythms somewhere north of two hundred beats per minute. Soaking wet and by anyone's standards irrefutably ripe, I unhinged. In a moment of clarity, I craved normalcy as an upstanding member of society. My main problem was my actions and aspirations never seemed to sync up. What was I to do? The answer came—heroin.

Heroin would bring me down to about fifteen beats per minute. I needed it like a kid needs a Slurpee. My heart had previously been clocked at two forty-seven by an unsympathetic emergency room nurse who eighty-sixed me from the hospital without so much as a Valium during a crack overdose. *Beat it scumbag,* had been her heartfelt prescription.

From deep within the bush, I locked eyes with the patriarch of a *Leave it to Beaver* type brood out for a leisurely stroll through the unnatural nature trails. I understood the patriarch's concern when he realized it wasn't a common feral animal indigenous to the eco-system that he'd spotted rustling around. The gig was up. It was me, down on all fours and covered in muck trying to ferret out a future for myself. Anything to furnish my rut.

With my cover blown, I needed to think fast, act casual and keep things light. I distinctly remember blurting a gem I will always cherish. "Man, you wouldn't believe some of the stuff people throw away. Really useful things." In a shooting gallery full of junkies doing their thing, it would have triggered some head nodding and all would've agreed. A little window, into the sexier aspects of addiction. By the lack of a response, it was obvious he considered useful to be subjective and had never been to a shooting gallery. I thought, *Man, what's eating him?*

Having no concept of self—shower or no shower, one shoe, no shoe, dead shoe, throw shoe—I've no doubt I would've used that gemmy as a pickup line if given the opportunity, but I never saw a suitable mate pass by. Grunge was all the rage in Seattle and at the time I was covered in it. Understand, it's not an excuse, just an explanation of the little slice of the under-life I'd carved out for myself.

Oh, the horror! You should have seen the looks on their faces. I'll tell you they stepped it up a notch. It was a classic Kodak moment. Saint Francis said, "It's better to understand than to be understood." What I understood was the time had come to blow the stink off and beat feet out of there before I started feeling justifiably weird about myself. I learned a valuable lesson: rock bottom has a basement.

Today, having been welcomed back to a new, cooties free existence, I don't have to check out or dig in a trash heap to hit pay dirt. All I've got to do is take it slow while clean, starched and ironed. Here in Paris—whoop, whoop—you wouldn't believe some of the things I've found on the sidewalks. Really useful things, like a two hundred fifty-year-old chestnut chair Terrell and I restored. A pair of Le Creuset cast iron tureens in pristine condition. Two disease-free hand-woven wool tribal rugs from one of the stan regions. A rare, red marble tabletop and lots of jewelry. There was one thing I found not to be so useful—the epic beat-down I fell victim to.

Louis XV era chair, before and after ressurection, with Terrell's silk brocade and down cushion. Not bad for what appeared to be a pile of rubbish.

Chapter 19
The View from Montmartre

Both my wife and I have always embodied a bohemian spirit. So, it's only logical that we landed in Montmartre where very little has changed.

I never get tired of looking out my window at the north side of Sacré Cœur.

There's plenty of history to consider in Montmartre. There's the cemetery, forever on the lookout for new recruits, where three hundred thousand former Montmartians have moved the fête underground. There's the last remaining Parisian vineyard, vintage 1933, which donates the proceeds from their annual seventeen-hundred bottle bounty to charity.

In addition to me, my wife and the Moulin Rouge, another one of Montmartre's shining stars is la Basilique du Sacré-Coeur, built on a plateau where cannons used to spit out eleven pound iron balls to defend the city. The base of Sacré-Coeur sits one hundred thirty meters above sea level and rises another ninety-one, making it the *true* pinnacle of Paris. As awe-inspiring as it is, according to one travel writer I read, "Due to the scam contingency who work the crowds, it is still considered a B-list Paris tourist attractions and better viewed from a distance."

Sacré-Coeur is a masterpiece of Romano-Byzantine architecture and the doors are open to all. There are regular services that run while the tourist crowd quietly makes their way around the perimeter of the inside. A ginormous Jesus-mosaic observes from above. There's also plenty of religious swag to be had. Almost as much as The Grateful Dead sold in their heyday, before Jerry died in rehab. So open up out those fashionable fanny packs and cough up a 10 € note to light a candle for Jerry.

The foundation stones were laid in 1874. Its completion came in 1914, just at the start of the Great War, WWI. What a celebration. Before the Great War there was the not-so-great Franco-Prussian War.

Basking in the hallucination that he was equal to his uncle, Napoleon III—the Edsel of Napoleons—put on his thinking cap and decided to invade Prussia. Napoleon II never got a chance to shake things up, he died of tuberculosis at the age of twenty-one. Nappy trois' forces were poorly trained and he had no natural allies. But as urban legend has it, he did want to make sure that the food was great, so he took a contingency of whisk-wielding chefs to the bloody battlefields. Surprise! He learned, never show up to a bayonet fight with a spatula.

When the dust settled, France had suffered casualties, six to one. To add insult to injury, the Prussian army encircled Paris and cut off the food supply, forcing Parisian chefs to serve up zoo animals.

This put an exclamation mark on the Franco-Prussian war and neutered the ineffectual, gout-stricken monarch for all time. Napoleon III might have fared better had he conscripted a battalion of Belleville butchers or some down and dirty Pigalle pugilists to enter the fray. The Kaiser then helped himself to the Alsace-Lorraine region, which has since ping-ponged back and forth, and after the treaty at Versailles, again became part of France.

Appalled by what a wuss Napoleon III showed himself to be, the people spoke, *"He ain't representin',* and took to the streets of Montmartre. Being the anarchist, socialist, artist, thug and prostitute capital of the Capital, Montmartre was the logical sight for a massive secular uprising. Woo-hoo! It must have been some kind of party.

Archbishop Guibert, a trembling but notable nabob, chose the location based on his vision to team up with the come one, come all wayward spirits and appease the Paris Commune. Sacré-Coeur was designed and built to help staunch the bleeding, the riots and the fires after his predecessor, Archie the Bishop, lost his head.

In the red-light district of Montmartre, worlds collide. The peace offering of a new basilica was a mastodon bone, thrown to the actionable anti-establishment sector that lived in the neighborhood. A place of worship they could call their own. Something they could be proud of during their Sunday morning pit stop to wash off the week's accumulated hedonistic residue. Could there be a more convenient place in Paris to be absolved of sin? Luckily for the masses, irony and a sense of humor are still alive and well.

Like pre-pandemic times, the flood of eager tourists pours into the Basilique to gauge the magnitude. Dusk is prime time for experiencing the magic of the divine dome. It's also prime hustle time for the African cowboys of Sacré-Coeur. These Eritrean rustlers—also known as the String Men—lasso mesmerized tourists with crafty macramé handcuffs, welcoming them back to the reality that the City of Lights sometimes goes dark. In the States, this would be called false imprisonment, as described in the Penal Code. Here in Paris, it's called a job. These guys don't seem dangerous, and although overpriced, their products *are* well made and provide a good story once safely back home. But their sales tactics are a bit brash. Still, it's an experience one could brag that they lived to talk about.

I ran into a neighbor on rue Caulaincourt. In the heat of the moment, he was getting belligerent with a condom machine that's attached to the facade of an ancient building. It had given him the short shrift by relieving him of his precious coinage. Thus, a fruitless mission. Condom machines are all over creation in Paris. While his window was closing, I said, "What you're experiencing is a luxury problem. You're blessed to have someone who's invited you into her sacred temple, the source of the universe. You may not be able to disappoint today, but you'll be back and apologetic before you know it." He took no offense to my ribbing. I asked, "Have you tried the one inside the Lamarck Metro?" All bases in Montmartre seem to be covered, in latex.

During Covid, the streets were mostly empty. Sidewalk cafés were but a fond memory and business was slim. A lone artist displayed his paintings of urban landscapes in the square. A smattering of maudlin, rain-soaked adventurers drank hot wine they'd purchased through the walk-up window, while pondering their mortality. Today the square is again teeming with life, love and mostly above board commerce. This colorful neighborhood begs to be explored.

In our apartment, painter Terrell prepares for photographer Terrell.

Terrell the photographer assists Terrell the painter.

MADAME J HAS A PET PROJECT

Here's another mini miracle geared towards acclimation. One day, my ultra formal neighbor Madame J. surprised me in the elevator by offering to give me French lessons. I accepted. When I asked her about payment, she waived me away.

She told me, "As a service to the country, I volunteer to teach immigrants the language." For three years, she had only smiled and said, *Bonjour* and *Au revoir* to me. I soon realized that her English is Oxford perfect after she corrected mine.

Her benevolence is even more remarkable as she is elderly and still works a full-time job. She lives in the apartment directly below us. It's a good thing I didn't buy that drum set at *La Baguetterie* that I so covet.

I'm a slow learner and when it comes to study habits, I have room for improvement. So much to do, so little time. I have trouble conjugating verbs—whatever that means—so she asked, "Didn't you learn proper grammar in school?" Just yesterday my wife said to me, "That's not a sentence. You need a noun." I didn't tell Madame J. that all I learned during my public education was smoking weed in the parking lot and then an indescribable language in gladiator school. The rest I learned by reading, so I said, "No," leaving out some of the detail. I believe she peered right through me and picked up on my angst all the way back to my childhood. She doesn't pry. She's very kind.

I've come to see her as a mighty force, of about forty kilos. When I get stuck on pronunciation, she gives me gentle verbal raps on the knuckles. I've spent twelve years of my life locked up and am more fearful of Madame J. than all the bone heads I was lumped in with in prison. I don't want to disappoint her. As my lesson night approaches the anxiety builds to absurd levels. I want to run away but I have no where to hide. Once the lesson starts—poof—I realize I'm having fun. The pattern has repeated itself week after week. As you've probably guessed, my angst has set up an Airbnb between my ears. She's since softened and has come to realize that as far as my studies are concerned, I ride the short bus. Sometimes I make her cookies. She approves.

She comes Monday nights for Terrell to prep her for the French citizenship test—which she has since taken and is now waiting for her thumbs up—and Wednesday nights for me, so I don't slip into obscurity. Terrell and I each sequester ourselves in the bedroom on the other's prospective lesson night. Turns out Madame J. has a robust sense of humor. I hear them wisecracking, imagining it's about my shitty level of French. I guess I'd better keep studying to find out.

Madame J. often commented on how beautiful one of Terrell's painting was. It was an oil and the first oil she ever painted. Terrell presented Madame J. with the painting after the one year mark of studies. Madame J. was blown back and accepted the gift with pleasure.

I'm not the only one who writes fiction. Madame J. was convinced I wanted to quit our lessons because she found a few sheets of completed homework in the recycle. What *she* saw was a garbage can overflowing with stacks of everything she'd ever brought over, cold slap in the face, meaning, I had no desire to continue. I talked her off the ledge by reminding her that we live in a cracker box apartment and must always be uber organized or we'd be buried alive. She accepted my explanation with affection and printed out another mondo stack of assignments.

She's proud of France and the French way of life and wants others to be proud too. Who can't get behind that? I'm proud to be taught by a person with a zest for the history and the language who isn't just yawning through the motions. Look closely and you'll find that France is crammed full of Madame J.'s.

Chapter 20
Balls and Noses

I was holed up in my Montmartre apartment pondering another snack while watching the exercise freaks out my window. This was before I sprained my ankle while listening to a friend brag about running the Paris marathon in three hours, seven minutes. I got a call from my dear friend who was out for her daily one-step-ahead-of-death senior citizen power walk. A walk I've been postponing.

She said, "Doug, there's a big, bearded guy laying on the sidewalk. He looks like Santa except he's wearing white painter's coveralls with the crotch blown out and he's really swollen."

That was alot of information. I wondered what she meant by swollen. I said, "Did he ask you what you want for Christmas?"

"No," she said, "I think he might be dead." In Paris, you're liable to see anything. "What do you think I should do?"

She's trusting to a fault but, as a three-decade veteran of the machinations of Paris, she's no delicate flower. And when push comes to shove, has no problem lashing out. Kind heart, sharp tongue. Stumbling upon a corpse wouldn't have surprised me. I'd seen a few in my prison days, but a swollen Santa? *That* disturbed me. I thought, *I'm no authority on such matters, but if it was me, I'd say a prayer, put a bag over my head and run like hell out into traffic.* But since I was a safe distance away and it was a moment of intense intrigue I said, "Are you sure? Better go have a look." Then I thought, *What have I done? I hope she keeps her distance.*

She concluded, "Not dead, he's snoring. I'm here with a group of women who've gathered."

"Ah! The buddy system."

"We're going to get him some help." I thought, *Way to go girls, that's the spirit*. Would I have loved to see what form that took. She said, "I'll have to call you back," as her team leaped into action.

A few minutes later, my phone pinged. She'd sent me a photo worth a thousand WTFs. Yes indeed, she'd spoken the truth. Porno Claus *was* swollen, not unlike the two grapefruits that had materialized after my double hernia operation. When I told her to have a look, I meant check his pulse or see if he could steam a piece of glass, not snap photos of his junk and contaminate my phone storage. I never said, 'I don't believe you, please send photos.' I'll never be able to wipe that image from my consciousness. I suspect some of her camera wielding cronies took liberties and flooded the dark web. She was trying to be nice and it got out of hand—who was it who needed help?

She followed up with another ping saying, "I called the cops." I wondered, *To turn yourself in?* Yes, she'd hung around a while. I knew she was retired, but damn. She'd approached the situation from a healer's perspective, as she had done that type of work. I just hoped she wore gloves. Thick, OSHA approved chemical gloves. If it all went sideways, I wouldn't be able to bail her out as my French negotiating skills are still laughable.

She reported back, "The cops roused him. He came to, argued, then started to masturbate."

"Perfectly natural," I said, "considering the state of his trousers. I must say, I was never that excited when the cops showed up for me."

Paris panhandling sign, "Too ugly for prostitution."

I recount this because I believe that today, I saw the shameless sidewalk Santa myself. Fortunately, not all of him, but enough of him to cede the space and walk in the middle of the street. For the moment, he's still drunk, but it looked as though Mrs. Claus had cleaned and stitched up his white jump suit and sent him out for an extended sidewalk safari.

Another sidewalk anomaly on *my* street is our low key—and to some, slightly pedestrian, but not entirely colorless—neighborhood clown. He wears no make-up or over-sized shoes. Nor does he speak. He whispers. This boyish, would-be gagster always has a knowing gleam in his eyes and carries with him a colorful collection of noses—fluffy, like pom poms, but look like litchi fruit—for all occasions.

I sometimes observe him from my seventh story window to gain perspective on human nature. I thought he might be a student on assignment.

Clown school is serious business here. One can earn a *Baccalauréat* +2 degree in France for clowning. Philipe Gaulier's clown school has taught many the art of physical comedy, Sacha Baron Cohen and Helena Bonham Carter to name a couple. The clowns of my childhood were J.P. Patches and his 6 foot 4 inch cross-dressing Raggedy Anne side-kick, Gertrude. They lived at the city dump.

Our clown—as I refer to him with my wife—has yet to bone up on the physical aspects of comedy. He stands stock still, fishing from a sidewalk where six streets meet a roundabout, for maximum traffic flow. His sole purpose seems to be impressing young women. To him, men are non-existant. He forever blows his high-frequency whistle, designed to entice a certain breed of young lovelies to stampede his way and bend to his will. One potential recruit approached wearing a Black Lives Matters T-shirt, so he swapped out his red nose for black and made his pitch. She muttered something scurrilous and kept moving without so much as a backward glance. Undeterred he finished his shift and showed back up the next day.

I ran into our beloved neighborhood clown on a cheek-to-jowl metro ride. We were standing next to each other. He was watching something on his phone and cackling unabashedly. I leaned in for a peek. Just as I suspected, it was a back-channel, freneticly disturbing cartoon clown video with plenty of blood and explosions. I fear he has now dissapeared into the bowels of Saint-Anne's psychiatric hospital for a chemical dumbing down and extended stay cure. If he does come back, we will always have a spot reserved for him on the sidewalk to work the crowd.

Chapter 21
Public Storage and the Dystopian Hellscape

Four and a half years after pulling the plug on our cushy but uncomfortable U.S. lives, my wife and I snuck back in to shut down our remaining storage unit. After five annual declarations of, "Hello valued customer, we're raising the rates, *again*. Thank you for choosing Public Storage," we swallowed hard and booked a flight back. Our nine-day working vacation was a frenetic week-long give away, and two days of bittersweet retrospection. Before arriving, our Seattle friends tried to prepare us for the bleak visual we were sure to absorb.

One morning before the sun came up in my Paris neighborhood of Montmartre, I noticed the hulks of several burned-out cars, satanic graffiti on building facades, tumble weeds, what appeared to be animal bones and plenty of garbage strewn about. All things evil had arisen out of nowhere. I was perplexed because things were quiet during the night. *What the flippin' heck?* Then I saw the film trucks and learned that the show, *Walking Dead Paris*, was in full production. A logical set location, considering we live down the street from Pathé studios, founded in 1896.

Monday morning, on our first post-pandemic trip through downtown Seattle, walking dead was also a thing. We drove one of the few cars on the road. Not quite a Mad Max landscape, but it did produce the vibe. The sidewalks too were just about empty, save for the occasional 8 a.m. doorway dweller chasing the dragon in the elusive pursuit of chemical joy. There was a bearded urban camper in a turn lane, hunched over his shopping cart, patiently waiting for the light to change.

I couldn't wrap my head around what was happening in one of the wealthiest spots on the planet. It could be a perfect storm of unaffordable rent, the Big Pharma Oxy debacle, cheap street narcotics, Big Tech moving in and gorging on all available downtown real estate, Covid-19 sending everyone in those downtown high-rise offices home to work and a fear-driven society at the edge of lost cause. At street level, much of downtown Seattle was boarded up and graffitied. The threat of arrest seemed no longer relevant. Open air drug use had become the new normal.

Our friend Kiki Erickson, sporting a Paris Plateforme du Bâtiment contractor's t-shirt.

I saw a young woman tromping with her beau, in a hurry to go nowhere. She spewed expletives and gesticulated wildly while on a fruitless quest I know very well. She had become so slight from her consumption she looked like a child wearing her daddy's cowboy boots and her mommy's skirt, as well as the face of her grandmother.

We got to our storage unit full of optimism and glad that we'd rented a safe, fifth floor climate-controlled unit. Our good cheer got snuffed out when we saw a worker making the rounds diligently bagging up mice from the fifth-floor traps. Our unit was full of surprises. Revisiting some of those forgotten treasures was a little bit like Christmas as a kid, when Santa was diabolical, and his reindeer had answered the call of nature. In addition to the mouse droppings, moths had—yum, yum—feasted on our precious Persian rugs.

No worries, I thought, *that's why we pay for insurance.* The storage company's claims adjuster thought, *No worries, that's why we make the fine print fine.* After filling their dumpster with what used to be our money, I did a quick internet search and found Public Storage would be more than happy to have me stand at the end of a very long refund line, in perpetuity. I sucked it up and let it go. Why not, everything else went.

Eighty percent of what wasn't damaged ended up in the hands of passersby, including Public Storage's designated mouse bagger to whom I gave a barely used, four hundred dollar Costco trampoline. He was jumping for joy. I told him, "You should wait 'til you get home and set that thing up." The rest went across the street to Goodwill. Tweakers stay plenty busy on that foul, one hundred yard stretch of road in an area known as The Jungle, which runs between Goodwill and the storage facility. Thirty some years ago, I too ran afoul on that jungle road.

Good news, the shippers arrived to gather up our non-negotiables. Bad news, I had no idea where we'd put it when it got to our tiny Paris apartment. The adventure continued. Subcontractors hired by the big boys arrived in a rental truck. The big boy's telephone call originated from Bulgaria, which I hoped was a suburb of Los Angeles, because that's where they claimed to be from when we hired them.

I'm not one to breathe down another's neck while they work and I didn't want to say out loud that I doubted the shipper's ability to deliver anything but fragments, but stacking a hundred-pound bronze sculpture on top of a box of breakables, then losing control and having it hit the deck before walking away to gather up another load, didn't leave me topped off with confidence. I hoped my supreme pre-packing job held true. The whole mess waved goodbye enroute to L.A. where it would be loaded onto a boat to Rotterdam and then onto a truck headed to Paris.

Postscript: Bulgaria was Los Angeles and what little we do still own arrived in A-1 condition. And with considerable organizing, did fit in our apartment. The last of the last. The cost of freedom, signed, sealed, and delivered.

The remnants of our belongings arrived in Paris.

Chapter 22
Banksy Hiding in Plain Sight

When considering architecture, food, clothing and art, pillaged and plundered, or produced onsite, Paris will always be the creative capital of the universe. It doesn't matter if we're talking about le Musée du Louvre—once home to the kings and government, but thanks to royal opulence, a citizen militia and the guillotine, now property of the *République*—or an Amorino ice cream shop, where cones are sculpted into perfect roses, I can't imagine there being a close second. I'm sure there are other places with a collective vibe and impressive museums one can visit to get a proper fix, but it's not necessary for me to venture beyond the city's border to get mine. Being in Europe where the whole world seems accessible, I am open to venturing to Egypt, Greece and Italy, but let me just cross Russia off my list.

Parisians cherish artistic expression. I buy a yearly Louvre pass and get to see things like groups of middle-schoolers on a Friday night tour, when it's not so busy. Kids hang with adults and soak it all in, and with pens and paper they have a go at replicating the masters. The only thing I soaked in on Friday nights at that age was chemically induced sweat and rejection.

You won't find Banksy's work stretched over a canvas. Not even at the Banksy Museum on rue du Faubourg Montmartre. All works there are reproductions and in no way tied to the artist, but nonetheless, popular with the tourists. I was clued in on the King Kong of guerilla artists unmistakable genius after watching the 2010 documentary, *Exit Through the Gift*

Shop. A film that he, she, they, it, wrote, directed and produced without detection. In the summer of 2018, my thirst for the real thing got quenched after I had the good fortune to go on a treasure hunt along with a handful of other fanatics. Banksy was on a tear in Paris. The art was hiding in plain sight and the paint was still wet. The more of Banksy's work I discovered, the more I recognized Banksy as a one of a kind, world-class artist and storyteller.

I thank *thelocal.fr* online magazine for dropping clues as to the whereabouts of some of the treasures, and to my wife for looking skyward at just the right time. On my pilgrimage, I noted that not everyone was bowled over or even aware of what they were seeing. This was evident by the shoppers who hustled, enroute to clean out Louis Vuitton or some other grotesquely priced accessory mecca. Footnote: Pre-Covid, being a paid L.V. shopper for the wealthy was a thing in Paris, because even the mighty Vuitton has limits on what constitutes greed. I exchanged locations and photos with the enlightened few I ran into who were also on the hunt. Across canal Saint Martin in the 19th arrondissement, a riff on the famous 1801 painting, *Napoleon Crossing the Alps,* was just a mile from my flat.

Protective plexiglass had yet to be affixed and graffiti on the graffiti had already begun. *Girl in a shroud* had been painted on a side door of the Bataclan nightclub, where part of the 2015 terrorist attacks took place. The door and girl have long since been poached. I found *Rat with a red polka-dot bow tie* about a block away from Shakespeare and Co., where I belonged to a Sunday night writers' group, until we—wasn't me, your honor—got kicked out for bad behavior.

Another rat, this time shot out of a bottle of champagne in the Marais, appeared around the corner from Mi Va Mi, which was my favorite, très affordable falafel joint until they decided to close their doors. Unfortunately, the rat and champagne bottle were considered vandalism. A graffiti removal contractor—who mistook himself for an exterminator—was called and only removed the rat.

A shrouded Napoleon Crossing the Alps. The paint was barely dry before it was tagged, hence the plexiglass.

Beware, Banksy has been known to replace graffiti removed with the likeness of the worker in the act of removing it. And lastly, as dumb luck would have it, there was a blindfolded rat riding a box cutter. The one discovered by my wife on the backside of a billboard in front of the Centre Pompidou where I used to scribe in the bibliothèque.

INTO THE LIGHT OF LE MUSÉE DE CLUMSY

Words of wisdom from a bumbling American tourist: if you're looking for anonymity in a thicket of spellbound pilgrims, let your transition lenses adjust from the 21st century glare before forging headlong into the dark medieval dungeon of the Musée de Cluny. The first thing I did was blurt, "Wow! What's that?" shattering a euphoric group trance with my vocal flare up. I'd been taken in by the past and made a beeline towards a wall-sized, six hundred fifty-year-old French oak relief sculpture.

Art from the Romanesque period was all about the dogma. Plus, the churches were the only ones with money—money which used to belong to the people—hence the frivolous art expenditures. Artists knuckled under and sold out for a bowl of porridge or found their heads on a stick. There were no robust, *au naturelle* women portrayed, ecstatic to be riding pillowy clouds while exposing themselves to the masses who fluttered by in flush admiration. The lascivious Rococo party was just an evil thought, still parked in the dark recesses of the future.

The gals depicted in the Cluny dungeon were hunched over beaten down scullions, painfully trussed up and scratching at black plague fleas. I doubt if even Jesus dared look at the sins of the flesh festering under those ghastly robes. As dominant and persuasive a figure as Diego Rivera was, if he'd been part of *that* scene, with his sassy mouth full of social commentary, he wouldn't have been able to sway the narrow oppressive thought train—even *with* a medieval Trotsky sidekick.

14th century music performed on replica instruments in the courtyard of the Cluny museum, Paris.

I tripped over the highly effective velvet dumb-dumb rope. "Jesus F...ing Christ," I bellowed, while landing sideways on the unforgiving oak floor. My family was so far removed from organized religion when I grew up, I really did believe that F...ing was JC's middle name. You'd think with all the wine the French guzzle, they could have at least made the floor out of cork. After one bruised tail bone and a red glow in the dark face, my transition lenses finally returned to normal. Too bad I never would.

When the other museum patrons came back into view, they dittoed JFC's look of anguish. A collective gasp filled the room. I felt empathy for all the ants being burned under little boy's magnifying glasses. It didn't bring the beatitudes, only the attitudes. I felt judged. Shame has a way of turning up the volume.

Where was the concern for *my* wellbeing? Everyone seemed concerned over that old chunk of wood. The guard remained stone-faced. The only muscle he *did* move was an eyebrow muscle, which said, *Good going, dipshit*.

Terrell seemed to care, "*Oh honey,*" she said, on the sad trombone end of the affection spectrum. I should have jumped into her loving arms but, feeling less than, I'd been contaminated by the funky vibe. It took a staggering dose of unconditional love for her to claim me. It is true, she can't take me anywhere.

I did a quick tally and concluded that I'd landed about a half meter away from splintering that old hunk of wood and working in perpetuity in the gift shop—or at least 'til the second coming—before I dusted off and slunk away to my next inevitable hiccup.

Let there be light. I'm happy to report that the Cluny has since been renovated. The space is well lit and inviting. And now the art appears to be safe from the likes of *moi*.

Chapter 23

French Crack and a Strong Note on Cheese

After about the fifth kid my wife and I heard screaming bloody murder, we suspected our little corner of Montmartre housed an absurd number of serial child abusers. *Should we call the police?* She relayed this distressing oddity to a friend, who asked, "Do you happen to live near a boulangerie?" Terrell said, "Why yes, right across the street."

Next episode, sure enough, a treat-deprived tot face planted on the sidewalk, enraged, pounding fists and blowing snot bubbles. While waiting for the malcontent to burn through the last of his disappointment vapors, the live-and-let-live parents carried on a conversation with friends as though they had no child at all. Their indifference appeared to fan junior's flames. It seems there are howling baby tantrum zones in front of every boulangerie—an effective advertisement for those condom machines.

Even though there are scads of boulangeries, Parisians aren't exactly tipping the scales. You won't find many elastic waistbands, motorized shopping scooters or SUVs backed up to the garage unloading from mega-stores. Most Parisians shop daily—on a trek for the freshest of everything. They ascend, flight after flight, up the spiral staircases to replenish their skinny Frigidaires. Paris is the only place you'll see a blinding fashion statement riding a bicycle with a three-foot-long baguette strapped to their back. Rail-thin Parisians trek from one boulangerie to the next, fueled by baguettes. There are ample residents in the city to support all the boulangeries without squeezing out the next guy. Many streets mirror each other with everything delicious one might need to sink their teeth into—a quilt of artisanal celebrations.

Once, I got lost two blocks away from our Airbnb apartment and had trouble spitting out my dilemma. The locals could tell even my English was wanting. I thought about yelling, *Help!* in the street, but instead telephoned my wife and threatened to turn myself in at the American embassy. I wouldn't have known how to find that either. I did find a café with a sympathetic waitress who dialed up my wife for me—I suspect I supplied a bit of merriment. The waitress sat me down with a basket of bread, comfort for my shattered psyche, until Terrell fetched me about five minutes later.

This was very confusing to me.

My wife is *sans gluten* (gluten-free) and eats almost no sugar, so I'm on my own. I can't seem to eat *pain au chocolat*—croissants baked with chocolate inside—fast enough. One thing I initially didn't understand was the short bags they put the baguettes in. I thought, *Are they trying to counterbalance all the paper wasted on bureaucratic redundancies or are the bakers just caught off guard by the potency of the yeast?* Based on all the street snackers, I determined that right out of the oven is the best way to enjoy a baguette to its fullest and it's rarely never right out of the oven. The bakery lines are long but move quickly, especially at lunch time, where a variety of sandwiches are just 5 €. Baguettes are baked all day and pastries all night. Seems the bakers never sleep.

Entries to the annual, *Concours de la meilleure baguette de Paris,* is an annual competition to determine the best in the city. Baguettes are judged on shape, length, weight, the crackle of the crust, evenness of the browned texture, softness of the inside and obviously flavor. Also, the mildly sweet and sour acidic fermentation of the yeast. It would be a hard task to judge.

Out of the fourteen hundred boulangeries in Paris, two hundred are judged by retired bakers, Jean Q. Publique, food critics and the bloggerati for best baguette. My old landlord said, "relationships can end over a bad baguette." Ours ended over something else. I stumbled upon a baguette vending machine in the south of France. I've yet to fully comprehend that one. The winner of the competition gets to put the official badge of honor in their window to funnel in customers. I'm always on the lookout.

Brebis, or not brebis, that is the questions. A sign on a *fromagerie* window read: "The cheeses are sleeping, please don't touch." If you want to be hit on the nose with an olfactory two-by-four, step inside any one of Paris's cheese shops. You'll be blown back by the cheese wizards' endless variety of sheep, cow and goat—don't worry, donkey milk is reserved for making soap.

A typical fromagerie window display.

You won't find any individually wrapped wood pulp products or aerosol cans dressed up as cheese stuff in France. And, if you bypass the conglomerates, you won't be able to get everything you want all the time. Some cheeses are seasonal, so the animals can claim their fair share of vacation time. Fromageries always have the freshest eggs. Big brown freckled eggs with pumpkin orange yolks that need no refrigeration because—that's right—eggs in France haven't been tampered with by diabolical food scientists and are admired on the kitchen counter for looks as well as taste.

I came late to the fondue party. I discovered that Roquefort isn't a gallon of Costco salad dressing, but a commune of cheese producers where the veined, moldy blue sheep's cheese originates. The town of Roquefort celebrates something that smells like ass but tastes way better. Don't be fooled by cheap imitations. EU law dictates that only those cheeses aged in the natural Combalou caves of Roquefort-sur-Soulzon may bear the name Roquefort. Cave-cured cheeses deliver a bold, punchier flavor. And the

EU law applies to Champagne on the wine side as well. The name of the product is also the name of the region. When it comes to food production, the French aren't to be trifled with. Counterfeit food production in Europe is a growing problem. If it's authentic you crave, make sure to look for the French flag on the label.

If all that doesn't sound too far out of your adventure zone, then you may want to take a step further with the seven stinky cheeses. Limburger comes in at number one. It's so strong you'll fight the urge to check yourself. Also, atop the putrid pinnacle sits Spain's Stinking Bishop—yes, another one—which is washed, not in the blood of the lamb, but in fermented pear juice. Gorgonzola, an Italien blue, also fits in there somewhere. Gruyère is the preferred fromage for *Soupe à l'oignon gratinée*. When submerged in the bubbling clay pot cauldron, it becomes rubber-band-like so beware, you could put an eye out.

I wasn't introduced to the world of cheese until I was well into adulthood. As a child, all I knew about cheese was that it was orange, puncture proof, wrapped in plastic and had no taste or smell. I have an ex-pat friend about to skulk back beyond the black stump into Wisconsin for a backwoods familial punishment hoedown. She promised to deliver a message for me. "Cheeses H. Crust, Brett Favre is a turd."

I paired my orange tasteless, fake cheese slices with white tasteless *Wonder Bread* and *Imbecile Whip*, because misery loves company. The trashy loaves were baked at the Hostess cupcake factory that was located on a notoriously dicey stretch of highway 99. I remember it as the corner of ho and Ho Hos. As an unsupervised pre-teen and with cheap entertainment hard to come by, I'd make the trek to watch the comings and goings of those cupcakes. *I believed that neither me nor the cheese would go bad.*

Une planche de fromage is on the dessert menu of many bistros. Individually, the French eat about twenty-six kilos of cheese per year. Raclette is a cheese fest originating in the Rhône-Alps region. A hard, whopping hunk of Swiss-type cheese is held over an open flame and scraped off to make campfire style grill cheese sandwiches. When sampling at a dinner party, the proper way is to start with the mild cheese and climax with the stinky, for full effect. Helpful hint: Don't be a numpty and lop off the tip of the wedge for yourself. Be kind, eat some rind.

Every *quartier*, or neighborhood, has plenty of small artisanal *fromageries*. The best ones have their own cool underground stone cellars where the cheese is stored. I live in a cheese laden neighborhood north of Sacré-Coeur. My favorites are the sheep and goat cheese from Chez Virginie.

On small-scale artisanal family farms, animal welfare in France is important, which is evident by the taste of the dairy products. As an animal loving food snob, I *always* opt for artisanal, to avoid the taste of fear. Our first apartment was directly across from a fromagerie. Not only did we shop there, but Terrell took French lessons from Madame, the proprietor. They read line by line out of a giant book, *l'Histoire du Fromage*. Terrell is now *très* cheese savvy.

Next to the Egyptians, Greeks and the Chinese, cheese is one of the most ancient cultures on earth. Fun fact: The U.S. produces about 26% of the world's cheese but exports almost none. If you're sharp, like cheese, I'll bet you won't lose sleep puzzling over that one.

Chapter 24
The Big Table

Because variety is the spice of life, common sense tells me my writing voice may not land on everyone's hedonic hot spot. I've teared up reading authors so good at capturing the human condition I thought, *I'm not fit to sharpen their pencils.* I've read others and thought, *Dang, where's my book deal?* Other than a heat rash from embarrassment, at sixty-five, I've yet to break out. But, glass half empty, I continue to write.

Writing is hard and this chapter may not escape death by blue pencil. *Is that the tolling of the bells I hear?* We shall see what my pragmatic editor has to say. I'm slowly leaning towards following directions over my worst instincts.

I'm not bitter about not having a seat at the big table, just a tad frustrated. But I am hungry, so I write like my stomach depends on it. Many writers write books, edition after edition, on how to write, plot or how to submit with a forward by another writer who also writes about writing, sometimes with the offer of an online Masterclass teasing delivery to publication's doorstep. There is no book on how to stare at the blank page or fly by the seat of your pants. Maybe I'll write one, *Rejection for Dummies.*

Many literary agencies have side gigs as paid consultants. An ethical gray area. There's always an army of fee-seeking strategists queued up, ready to pounce on the insecurities of an unpublished author. Admittedly early on, I opened my wallet and fell with glee into a couple of those dark, unproductive crevices. But then again, I used to smoke crack, so it wasn't that bad.

When asked, "What do you do?"

I say, "I'm a writer," because I like the way it glides off my tongue.

After the silent question, *But how do you live?* hangs in the air, I say, "I work as a carpenter to pay the bills."

I won't say I don't want people to read my stuff, I do. But with smartphones and so much visual bombardment, it's a hard sell to expect people to sit quietly and read a book when there's so many important snippets of information to sift through.

I really thought that after I put my book *Fixed* out there, I'd be a shoo-in for an interview with Terry Gross—an obsession that, for a couple of years, would not leave me alone.

There's plenty of rejection to go around in the land of the unagented writer. When I do finally rise to the top of the slush pile and get sloughed off, I tell myself rejection is protection and what people think of me is none of my business. I feel very much protected while feeding the rejection machine.

This book isn't just about how I got here, but also what I do here. Since arriving in France, in addition to running my one-man construction business, I've written three novels and this kitchen sink memoir, all languishing on my desktop in search of a safe harbor. As the calendar pages flitter away, I comfort myself by looking at the criminally short list of writers who broke in late, which almost sounds like a burglary. Frank McCourt and Laura Ingalls Wilder's names are often bandied about. Do I dare dream that my name will one day be put forward? Why not.

There's only one way for me to rise above the slush pile, and that's to expose myself with words on a page. Perhaps this sounds like a no-brainer for the emotionally balanced, but when it comes to feelings, I had to start over after two plus decades at the chemical checkout counter. Then there was prison, where being vulnerable did bring many closer, but only half by choice.

In the real-world school of feelings, I've unpacked more than just anger and fear. Now feelings are plentiful and far-reaching, a rolodex ready for all occasions. And then there's language. I may be learning French, but I'm also still learning English—which twenty years ago I spoke with a Neanderthal, big yard accent. Why the twisty road to illumination and not a stark white light?

Post sobriety, voracious reading has helped me embrace English as a first language. The streets and prison yards have their own bastardized versions which takes years to learn and are not without merit. At forty-two, after my lost decades, I snuck into college. My English Professor told me, "Your words are strong, you just need to juggle them a bit. And a period now and again wouldn't hurt, either." Good advice. I wrote it down.

I've sent manuscripts to many publishers and some weeks later got slapped down with, "Dear Author..." My name died with their interest. Whether they like me or not, I continue to float them out there, like a message in a bottle. Sometimes it seems like a comedy routine. I'll hold off on the back flips until I decide what constitutes success.

A trusted reader told me the first draft of my first novel was, "...a crowded bus and not one I'd care to take a ride on." After a good man cry, I broke all my pencils and went on a character assassination spree, giving birth to a new, leaner, more inviting cast of characters who I've since killed and replaced.

I've read my material to a group of drooling, moon-gazer poets, who didn't give a rat's ass what I said. They were too busy trying to escape their own awkwardness. I crashed and burned so spectacularly in their dead eye sockets, that I had to send an imaginary ground crew in to collect my black box. I went to bed that night needing a pacifier. I thought, *I suck*. When I woke up, I sucked a little bit less and wrote a little more.

I once asked a writer friend who's enjoyed some success, but retired to bask in past glories, "Do you have any advice that might be useful?"

"Yeah," she said, "don't ever expect to be a successful writer." She said this not because she's read any of my work and considers it pap, but because she believes the publishing field has reached capacity and it's all been said. She may as well have said, go fuck yourself. In French, that would be considered a reflexive verb. *Je me baise*—I fuck myself. 'Hey, thanks for the great advice,' I said, before taking a four-day nap.

I've been fortunate to make connections here in Paris that I wouldn't have been able to make elsewhere. Things unfold and I make my pitch. In the long list of notables, I managed to cozy up to Frédérique Dumas, who sprang for my tea and wanted to talk about my book, *Fixed*. I didn't even have to use my dormant weasel skills, it just happened. Who is she? She's a Representative in the Halls of French Congress—*Assemblée Nationale.* At that time, she was also *Directrice Générale* for Orange film and television studio. A modern-day Louis B. Mayer, without sexual harassment baggage. And she didn't come across as someone who forced people to take drugs and work long hours during production.

There's an old German guy I sometimes rub shoulders with—a retired White House correspondent who wrote for *Der Spiegel*. I told him I was a retired crack house correspondent and offered him some of my aged headlines. He took a pass. I bumped into a Hollywood A-lister, who's portrayed guys like me on the big screen. We got to talking and he gave me his phone number. He said, "Call me and we'll talk about your books. I've got a friend who owns a publishing house." I called him, he didn't answer, I let it go.

I met another Hollywood A-lister, who will go nameless because I don't want to be associated with a Me Too cancelation. After sharing that he'd just skied Chamonix, he asked me, "What are you doing in Paris?" I told him I was writing. He said, "Do tell." I whipped out a copy of *Fixed* I just happened to be carrying around, signed and gifted it to him. I'm sure the call from his agent will come through after he repairs his reputation. David Sedaris and I swapped signed copies of our books. He said, "*I never got a Kirkus starred review.*" Too bad you can't spread an attaboy on a cracker.

Shameless self-promotion for my book, Fixed.

Chapter 25

Locked Out

In the Upper Rainier Beach neighborhood of Seattle, break-ins fueled the anxiety of life in the hood. The prospect of being ripped off was ever present and all too real. I once blockaded a car full of felonious punks with my pickup truck, as they conspired in my driveway. I got out, snapped a photo of them and their license plate, then sent them on their way. They accepted defeat, shrugged their shoulders and moved on to easier pickings. My killer guard dog, Zinc, snoozed comfortably through the whole episode.

I once chased a burglar down the street with a framing hammer. I'd spotted him rummaging around in my octogenarian neighbor's house. In my proud, well-kept working-class neighborhood, we neighbors vowed to keep an eye out for each other and report any suspicious activities. Lost on me was that a hammer is no match for a gun and based on the steady stream of muzzle reports, there were plenty.

In Paris, things are a bit more relaxed. The apartments are built with thick blocks of stone and are *très* secure. Keypads are necessary to breach the multiple entrance doors, a difficult assignment for sinister elements. If someone does manage to break through the first layer of security, they're caught loitering in a burglar's no man's land. My current apartment has five locks. Typical for Paris, one's operable and self-locking when you pull the door closed, and four are for show. All this to say, don't go out of a Paris building without your keys, because you'll be hard pressed to get back in.

And to get out, one must hunt for the button on the wall that allows the door to open. Sometimes it's not so obvious.

"If we ever lock ourselves out, what should we do?" I asked a couple we know.

"Identify a good locksmith before you need one," they said, "but make sure they're a member of the locksmith association and ask for credentials." They had the experience of paying four hundred euros to gain entry back into their flat through the splintered door jamb that Smithy had put his boots to. I've heard similar stories about pseudo-locksmiths taking hostages and demanding ransoms. They feast on the desperation of those locked-out. Fear of a night on the streets in Paris can cause blind trust. No key, no receipt, happy to be of service. A reputable locksmith is in the one hundred fifty range without all the shrapnel.

It was a starry night on the Seine, perfect for art exploration at the Musée d'Orsay. When my wife and I returned to the entry door of our building, we realized we had no keys. We also had never identified a good locksmith. We sped back by cab to the museum with the thought that they'd fallen out when she sent her bag through the metal detecting conveyor belt. The empathetic protectors of the art let her back in at closing time for a quick look around. They must have caught a whiff of my thieving residuals because they had no love for me, so I just gave her two thumbs up from the other side of the villain proof windows.

She retraced her steps, scouring the museum for the lost keys. *Rien*. We limped off in no particular direction into the cheerless night. My wife, not familiar with what creeps after dusk said, "This is fun! We can just walk around and stay up all night!" Having been homeless in a big city and on the opposite end of trustworthy, I warned her of an element I knew all too well, me. "Absolutely not" I said. We trudged on.

No vacancy was the verdict in every hotel we came across, a sign would've been helpful. I felt dirty, tired, suspicious and accident-prone.

My wife pointed to a fetching sign, "There's one!" We stepped into the lobby. It sported a fashionable Japanese motif, with a wall of foliage and a water feature. "Yes, we have a nice suite available. Would you like to put it on your card?"

"It fits on a card, how much?" Neighborhood to neighborhood, there's quite a contrast to hotel prices in Paris.

"Sixteen hundred, per night."

"Yen?"

"Euros."

How much for a mop closet?

I felt a splash of regret over the fiver I'd tossed at a guy wrapped in a blanket on the sidewalk. I said, "Let me check with my shorts," and pivoted on my heels. We were on Rue Saint-Honoré, where scads of major fashion houses pimp their wares. So, I asked myself, *Where would I not be willing to live in Paris?* The answer was, *Next to any one of the seven deadly train stations.*

The Metro was about to close for nightly defunkification, so we had to act fast. "Honey, let's find a train station." We went underground and came out on the blade at Montparnasse. There was an assemblage of barely clad, reasonably priced humans, in all shapes and sizes. Men, women and hybrids, ready to receive and service customers. We also found an affordable hotel. The stone-faced attendant fixed us up with an on the surface fresh, red velvet, bed bug-free room—we went through our protocol—for two hundred a night. Exactly what we paid for a five star in Lisbon.

After a dubbed *Columbo* rerun and a short nap we ran like we stole something back through the sleeping red-light district of Montparnasse. We needed to get on the Metro and make it back to our building before 8:30 a.m., when Madame Spare Key who lived three floors above us would leave for her appointment.

I'd made a friend by sharing pastries with the young man who worked at the tool rental shop two floors below our apartment. It's where carbon monoxide from all the gas-powered machinery being tested poisoned us in our second story walk up. The necessary remedy to our conundrum was that he let us pass through the side door of the tool shop, which allowed us to bypass two security doors and huff and puff our way up to the fifth floor for the spare key.

After catching our breath, I listened to my wife, an American immigrant and Madame key holder, a Bulgarian immigrant make French small talk before we got what we came for. The good news was we didn't lose the key. We'd just left home without it.

Later—though I was not immediately sprung on the idea—we sprang for an expensive box of chocolates as a thank you and to grease the wheels if there was ever another episode. Desperation is the mother of all willingness.

Chapter 26

Le Tour, all Over the Map

My first bike ride was on a borrowed Schwinn Stingray. With the sound of someone else's baseball cards whirring as they hit the spokes, I careened down a hill, over a rockery and through a plate glass window—a forecast for things to come. *Howdy neighbors!* I had arrived.

I was six and didn't know squat about brakes. Cheryl Liedtke—also six—told my mom that I'd near cut my hand off and it was dangling by a piece of skin. Curious, she parked her crossword to investigate. This was twenty-four years before I really did almost cut my hand off. I was operating a skill saw in the dark. I did alot of things in the dark. The bike accident required multiple stitches but nothing more. I couldn't wait to do it again.

My first experience riding a bike in France was at the Palace of Versailles, which was less suicidal than before Covid, when there weren't so many bike lanes. Bikes come in handy at Versailles because the palace grounds are so expansive, one could spend a whole day wearing out their Gucci loafers just trying get somewhere.

Late July is the time of year Parisians go on vacation and follow the last Tour de France rider right out of town. Those left behind are forced to fight over the sole remaining chicken bone because a lot of the stores are closed. I may lose those two extra kilos yet. Leaving Paris to go on vacation is a concept I can't wrap my head around.

The real heroes of the sport are those daily comuters, all spruced up and enroute to their dreary cubicals while navigating the dangers of the skinny Paris streets. The every day cyclist doesn't get sponsorship or escorts passing off energy drinks and potassium packed bananas to stave off leg cramps. And since the streets aren't cordoned off, they might just get clipped by a taxi. They embrace death free of charge.

I tried watching part of one of the legs—the thigh, I think—of the Tour de France on *la télé*. After the name had changed to *le Tour de Lance*, just before it was thought of as *le Tour d'Enhance*, some joker named Thomas won the race. I'm sorry I can't be more specific than that.

Transporting tools from the Latin Quarter to Montmartre on Boulevard de Sébastopol.

Twenty-three days and over two thousand miles of, *What the hell am I doing this for?*, finishes through the Arc de Triomphe. It takes three weeks for the grandstands to be build, a couple of hours for the hundreds of riders to whiz by and three more weeks to tear the grandstands down.

I never rode two thousand miles, but I did run eight miles in Yakima, Washington with a stack of pilfered Levi's tucked under my arm. I hopped the fences of man-eating-beast-filled backyards, to escape the relentless pursuit of the strapping female security guard tasked with suspending my animation as a plunderer. I too, had plenty of training and was highly motivated.

I have a rabid-biker brother back in Seattle that I needed to wrestle some swag for near the finish line. I knew it would be me and a million other hopefuls, mudwrestling for freebies along the Champs-Élysées. So, at the end of le Tour, I weaseled my way up front, just past Place de la Concorde, for a bird's eye view of the last foot of the last leg as one skeletal rider after another crossed the line back to sanity. I could see every vertebrae pass by. The Italian team tossed me one of those tiny caps, like the one AC/DC's seventy-year-old guitarist Angus Young wears to appear boyish. Small hat. Big head.

I'm no reporter, but oh how I wanted to interview Texan and last place finisher, Lawson Craddock, the hero of the Tour. He was such a badass, he rode nineteen hundred miles with a broken collarbone and an angry gash above his eye. A spectating dildo rolled a strike by skittering his water bottle across the road, causing a massive pileup, But Craddock managed to finish the race and, in my mind, steal the show.

During Covid, things were subdued. When the sun's shining and the city is bloated with tourists, it's impressive to witness all forms of transportation on the Paris streets jockeying for pole position. Bikes, motos, cars, buses, trottinettes, electric skateboards, electric uni-wheels towing suitcases, rollerblades, granny with a walker, etc. This mania sometimes results in multiple mode accidents, with the loser on the ground looking up at the winner, who looks down to pin blame. I got hit by an electric trottinette in a crosswalk. The commuter indicated it was my fault by yelling something like, *Watch where you're going, baldy!*

Paris Mayor Anne Hidalgo is a socialist's socialist and my kind of gal. She's been Mayor since 2014 and has implemented many green planet-friendly programs such as, *Paris Respire*, or Paris Breathes. No more cars will be allowed in certain areas of the city on Sundays. And soon, no more dirty diesel within the city limits. The only dirty diesel allowed will be Vin. Anne encourages all of us to get off our duffs and ride.

When I got here, I only rode the Metro and was plenty freaked out by doing just that. But riding the Metro robbed me of the beauty above ground and tricked me into thinking that geographically, the city was much larger than it is. It also prevented me from seeing how it all connects. Mayor Anne cut swaths from all the streets and designated them as bike lanes, with more coming all the time. After seeing a bus-bike accident, I swore it would be the death of me if I mounted a two-wheeler. But I've dodged death before and when Covid hit, I put on my training wheels and became one of the maniacs I used to rail against. For a guy who once pined to wear a toe tag, it turns out there's still plenty to see above ground.

Terrell kickstarting our garden with what turned out to be fragrant and flourishing roses.

For about one hundred euros, I get access to Paris' Vélib brand electric bikes for a year. On some days, the upright sturdy bikes are a good deal. The high-rent neighborhoods have plenty of bikes but no empty stanchions to park them. The working class hoods have no bikes, but plenty of parking spaces. I work and shop for materials on a bike. I also transport large tools on a bike, courtesy of the roomy baskets and bungie cords. You name it, I ride with it.

Vélib customer service seems to have only one employee because I reach the same guy every time I have a problem. We recognize each other's voice. Last time we chatted I said, "Eight minutes into my ride to pick up supplies my peddle fell off. I've been all over hell trying to unload this f..king bike. With one leg." I was wrapped around the axle.

He said, "Please don't swear sir."

I said, "Dude, I know you. This is Piotter."

He started to laugh and said, "I thought I recognized your voice. Let's find you somewhere to park."

I said, "If I wanted to walk, I wouldn't have checked out the bike." He considered my position and let me lock it to a post, right where I stood. I'm now one with the flow.

Pampered Parisian pets.

I reached a point while riding where I let my guard down and became too comfortable. I T-boned a taxi and bounced off the driver's door at about twenty-five miles per hour. The Japanese driver was hotter than a wasabi fart. He cussed me up and down in his native tongue. I don't believe he was truly mad, just a bit scared. If I'd have been riding just a bit faster, I wouldn't be writing this now. With adrenaline pumping I offered a thousand apologies and kept moving. I have a strong will to live so I've since toned it down. Please don't tell my wife.

Bikes in Paris have now overtaken cars as a preferred mode of transportation. I can ride from my apartment north of Sacré-Coeur to Galignani bookstore—the first English bookstore on the continent and dead center of the city on Rue de Rivoli near the Seine—in sixteen minutes. In Paris, daily trips by bike outnumber daily trips by car almost three to one. Sometimes the police ride horses in the bike lanes. Dodging their offerings slows things down considerably.

When Olympics mania took over the city—*Allez les Bleus!*—Place de la Concorde wasn't accessible to any mode of transportation, other than Olympic skateboarders. Ten-million visitors converged, but they must've all been in the venues, because I didn't see many of them on the streets, except during the cycling road races which ran right through my neighborhood.

The one hundred thirty-five year-old windmill blades of the Moulin Rouge fell off three months before the start of the Olympics. There was a major push to refurbish before the opening ceremonies, and Paris delivered. The new blades are brilliant and light up the night. When the Olympic cyclists passed by the Moulin Rouge, the Cancan girls were out front, high kicking and in fine fashion. During the Olympics, the city was clean and serene while the French were out of town complaining elsewhere, until they snuck back in to catch the vibe and witness the miracle.

BRUNO'S THE MAN

Grumbling aside, the French are proud of their country and all that it represents. And they want others to be proud too. The French I've come to know go all in to help foreigners integrate, so long as they're sincere. That's been my personal experience, especially with Bruno.

Bruno is a people person and always ready to tackle a problem. He's knowledgeable and connected, just the type of person Terrell and I needed to meet upon arrival to help point us in the right direction. We were having trouble making an appointment to renew our visas. Our *récépissés*—the paper placeholder one gets until called in to pick up the official laminated visa—had expired and we'd been officially out of bounds for some time. We were sitting at an outdoor café when, indignant on our behalf, he whipped out his phone and said, "I'm calling the Chief of police." The Chief told him, "Covid has backed things up. Sorry, but they'll have to wait their turn like everyone else. Tell them not to worry, it's normal." We *had* been fretting. The Chief's statement put us at ease.

Bruno made the bold move because he genuinely appreciates our desire and drive to live here and become French. And he knows the Chief. Bruno holds us up as examples for others. *Just look at them go!* Sometimes when he insists on intervening in this or that difficult situation, I say no, you're doing too much for us already, but he always insists. He says, "It is the French way, do not deny me what is right."

While apartment hunting, Terrell and I discovered that since we're not wealthy, or young, or hold government jobs, we needed a signer to rent an apartment. No matter that we were clearly able to pay our own way and had built a two-plus year track record here of paying on time.

Bruno asked me, "How's it going with the apartment hunt?"

I said, "We finally found one, but we need a signer."

Without hesitation, he said, "I'll be your signer."

Uneasy, we discussed it with an expat friend who's been here decades. She said, "You're applying your American value system to a foreign country. France is relational, this is how they do things here." Because homeless wasn't something we aspired to be, only a bone head wouldn't except help under such circumstances. We heard what she said and decided to accept help. At the end of the month I sometimes jokingly tell him, "Sorry Bruno, I'm broke, you're going to have to pay my rent."

Chapter 27
Thalasso Fiasco

My mom used to wear these little plastic rain bonnets to protect her freshly permed and lacquered helmet of hair from the dark clouds that perpetually followed us Piotters around. She'd hoof it on unstable stilt type shoes from the beauty salon to the Rimrock Steak House, her favorite drinkery, and uncork herself for a twelve-hour shift of lights out drinking with the skeezy urban cowboy club. They fit inside a clear plastic pouch. The bonnets, not the cowboys. I remembered this as I opened the pouch of my *Boxer de Bain* swimwear, miniature swimwear I was forced to shoehorn myself into on my four-day adventure at a Thelasso Spa Resort in Brittany. The French are mad about spas. *It's just water, for cryin' out loud.*

France, a modest Catholic country, is all about conformity. All spa pilgrims milled about in thick, full-length white terrycloth robes. But once inside the sacred sanctum—bam!—off came the terry cloth and *in your face* with the horrors of old age. I said to my wife, "Let's get out of here."

After being reprimanded for trying to contaminate the pool with my abominable American swim trunks, I was forced to purchase their snug signature swimwear. My deep-seated suspicion of vulture capitalism kicked in.

The enforcer said, "We'll put them on your room." She meant my tab. I said, "That'd be great, 'cause I'm not wearing 'em." My repartee got lost in translation and died somewhere over the Atlantic.

I told my wife, "Just you wait, there'll be all kinds of bogus, indecipherable charges tagged to the room." I thought to myself, *Why, oh why? Nobody wants to see my junk.* Then I thought, *What a shame.* With such skimpy pieces of fabric, who could look away? It's automatically where all eyes go to linger.

At that point I went back to the hotel room and opened the package. And like an infant in front of a bakery, threw an epic tantrum. I did my best Gloria Swanson, tossing my robe on the floor. I held the back of my hand across my forehead and told Terrell, *"I'm not wearing these!"* referring to the spandex panties. I held them over my head and stretched the resistance trained fabric—"Grrraahhhh!"—with all my might. I thought, *We might as well be at a nudist colony.* Even a he-man workin' his pecs at muscle beach couldn't have prevented those trunks from snapping back into form. Impressive chemistry.

My wife said, "Little-known secret, it's what all the straight men wear in France." Victor's secret. In prison, they'd be referred to as man-catchers. I thought, *Man, I'm sixty-two, it's a little late to be auditioning for the other team.* After I flamed out, I conceded and donned the freakish swimwear. Just as I suspected, like the eyes of a portrait that follows you around the museum, everywhere I went an endless stream of water-ninnies spied me. I thought they were called privates, not publics. There's nowhere to hide from the critical eye.

People are at their most vulnerable when they're practically in the scud. I would have given my left nut for a little modesty, but I'd already given it, by way of a botched hernia operation, while in prison. My friend asked me to take some pictures of the facility, but I wasn't exactly wearing cargo pants, so where to stash my phone was another dilemma.

No free thinkers allowed. There are rules to be followed, so park your imitation Voltaire at the door. I was scolded for saving a lounge chair. It was first come, first serve and hair must be tied up. Being bald was my lone savored victory. Even though the security guard/water aerobics instructor spoke in French, what I heard was a Hitler speech, because I pegged her for a pool Nazi, and my *Boxer de Bains* dictated I hate her. My pushback and paranoia finally dissipated.

Since the trip was supposed to be about what my wife wanted after I'd strapped her to the power tools on a four-month construction project, I was forced to be a good sport and subject myself to a menu of humiliations. First up on the spa treatment list was a fifteen-minute saltwater hose down by a wannabe fire fighter. Necessary if I were a moldy cedar deck but, c'mon. I flashed back to 1978 when I was in the buff, leg ironed to nineteen other naked lottery winners and chemically water-cannoned on my way to a first felony award. They didn't want us to introduce any foreign elements into such a pristine environment. Oh what fun I was in for. That episode stung in more ways than one.

Next up, I was handed what looked like a black Covid mask for newborn Siamese twins. I was instructed, "Put this on."

I thought, *Where? How?* Reading my mind, she shrugged and said, *"Je reviens tout de suite"* and skipped out. Thongs are something to be worn on the feet. I may have put it on backwards. It still haunts me. My self-awareness was doubly acute, but the fabric of my disillusion had shrunk to a new low, just half a rung north of porn. I prayed I'd hit my bottom.

The twenty-something female came back in with her smirk and a bowl of hot mud to wipe down my entire landscape. I was petrified. While I was in the shower washing off the lumps of shame, she popped back in to pose a question, "Do you need some help?" I wondered, *What kind of help are we talkin'?* I need a lot of help, but on that occasion, I took a pass.

The cosmic undulating waterbed jet tub was as over the top as an eighteenth-century puffy shirt. The pulsating disco beat emanating from the French hipster sound system added misery to the mystery of where I might be headed. Might I be swallowed and spit out in an underground parking garage? Or inserted into a Matrix-style pod cluster? I assumed all that would be extra and also tagged to my room. My mind was a runaway train.

Madmoiselle masseuse came back in and slapped me with another thong. One minute in and my foot had a seizure before she got a chance to get her hands on me. She interpreted my spasm as the white flag of fragility and thankfully, the massage was over before it started. No discount for you, said the taxing apathetic universe.

ANOTHER SHINING MOMENT IN MENTON

While traveling and staying in hotel rooms I'm cautious and always make use of the room's safe. It's the prudent thing to do. I don't know if I had a flare up from my everyone's-out-to-get-me cocaine psychosis days, it was a Covid hangover, or God forbid, it's the direction I'm heading, but on day two, in a fine and reputable establishment which I stayed at the year before, I took an erroneous detour.

The safe was black. It sat on a shelf above a mini black fridge. My wallet is also black. There was a dark space between the safe and the fridge, about the size of the one between my ears. There were two things about the room that were not perfect. One, the cradle for the hand-held shower wand was broken, so one either needed to tie it off with something or soap up and take a shower with one hand. My wife chose to tie it off—she does not remember doing so—since it was the week of *Fête Nationale* and a repair was unlikely to happen 'til after August when France returned from its six-week vacation. I took a photo of it and informed the young woman on night duty so they wouldn't assume I broke it.

My favorite baroque cathedral is in Menton, a short walk to the Italian border on the Riviera.

The village on the sea is not inundated with vipers, vultures or pirates, and the hotel staff was helpful and friendly. And I recognized them from the previous year. It was a vacation I'd been saving for since I'd stayed the year before. The second thing that tilted my axis was that only the numbers 2 and 0 were functional on the safe's digital display. This was when the ersatz conspiracy took root.

I crammed all my valuables into the safe, punched in 0202, put the *Do not disturb any further* sign on the door, and it was off to the beach. And not just any beach, but the azure waters of the French Riviera in Menton, half a mile from Italy. Upon my return to the hotel room, I panicked.

"Where's my wallet? Somebody stole my wallet. I'm not kidding," I told my wife. "It was in the safe when I left!"

"Take a breath," she said. "We'll find it." She started her own, methodical, drama free, dickhead free search, while—like a fish out of water—I flung about, sifting through our belongings and freaking out. "Give it five more minutes before you go down," she said. I noticed deep crevices carved in her forehead. Did she mean, *In flames*?

Being the instant gratification impatient guy that I am, I spouted, "I'm going down now."

"Funny," she said, "I don't remember tying off the shower head." Her moment of doubt was all the confirmation I needed that I'd been had. Convinced someone had been in the room, off I went with phone in hand, ready to point my holstered fingers. Doesn't every burglar tie off the shower head before ransacking and making an escape?

Two beatific women, the older proprietor and a young staffer, greeted me. I wasted no time grilling them. I panted like a dog while I barked out my accusation. "Take it easy," the proprietor cooed, "we'll scroll through the surveillance video, before we call the police."

Being one who, on multiple occasions, has donned the stainless-steel bracelets, I didn't like the sound of that. Nonetheless, I hung on to my accusatory bone. I told her what time my wife and I had left and watched while she rolled the tape. Sure enough, someone came out of my room. I took a vicious stab at the air and spit out, "Look! There he is, I told you so!" Then said. "No, wait, that's me."

I complain mightily about not getting phone calls, but my ringer is perpetually off. By that time my wife had called me three times. She rounded the corner to the front desk waving my wallet like a white flag. That's when I really hoped I had lost my wallet. Funny thing, no one was mad, except me. I hyperventilated and fell hard on my sword. A million apologies ensued. "I am an immigrant," I said to the proprietor, which had no bearing on anything. "Do you remember me from last year?" I asked, trying to soften their opinion of me for insinuating they were all a bunch of thieves.

"No," she said. I reckoned she would next time, if I dared show my face again. I looked for an armadillo shell to crawl inside of. "Can I get you a coffee, or maybe, a water?" Like a cookie for a crying baby, she brought me a fancy bottle of Italian spring water, on the house.

In my haste to get to the beach, I pulled my computer out of the safe with my wallet on top. I rearranged everything, neat and tidy and put my computer back in. My wallet had slipped off to the far reaches of the black void between the fridge and the safe.

I've witnessed prejudiced folks who train their wary eyes on people they suspect are out to get them. Please don't let me become one of those old-paranoid-farts who suspects everyone is out to pinch him when he misplaces his marbles.

Even though I'm always certain, I'm not always right, I truly do believe most people are good.

FRIENDS ABOUT TOWN

Troy, former loose cannon, modern-day mensch, is a friend who grew up in my era and has lived a similar life. He too has been gifted grace, so I'm naturally drawn to his orbit. He may be the only guy who ever stole from the Boston mafia and lived to tell the story. They went so far as to put him in the back seat of a car to work out a payment plan. He thought, *Time to pay the reaper, I might not get out.*

Troy is a painter, writer, musician and film maker, with a splash of carnival barker. He oozes creativity and unconsciously knows how to sell himself, something which doesn't come naturally to me. With zero hesitation, he flings his fervor at those he encounters and beyond. At his street-side workspace he leaves the door open for a steady stream of curious

Montmartre tourists to pop their heads in, which sometimes pays dividends. If he was a light fixture he'd be covered in moths. But he's a painter, so instead he's covered in paint.

I was with a large group of Americans having lunch at an outdoor café. My group of four parked ourselves outside, after being bullied to give up the table next to us for folks more important. Troy's group of five skulked inside. My group ordered. Time passed. Troy was still lit up from the successful first showing of his debut film, *A Matador in Paris,* at a tiny but jam-packed Art Deco theater in the 9th arrondissement the night before. The pendulum swung.

There was a flap from inside heading our way. Troy squawked, "What do you mean you're kicking us out?" There'd been a misunderstanding. One of his tablemates claimed he didn't receive what he'd ordered. Troy floundered, his eternal glow, snuffed out. In defense of his erroneous tablemate, he said, "The guy doesn't even speak French." He pointed at the waiter who'd brought our food. "He's kicking us all out for something I did seven years ago when I was drunk. It wasn't even at this café!" He stabbed the air, "This guy's crazy!"

I said to Troy, "And to think he could've gotten your autograph." I felt bad for razzing the ballistic showman, but my filter is sometimes leaky. He walked away hungry and mumbling indignities with four bewildered tourists in tow.

In the spirit of solidarity, I had a fleeting thought of walking away, which cleared my conscience. The waiter showed back up with our food and with an air of self-righteousness said, "I'm not crazy, you know."

I shrugged and said, "I have no opinion, I have the soup."

Chapter 28
Academy of Grift

After I took a voluntary nineteen-month "cure" in a Washington State Department of Correction's safe haven, my mental compass pointed me towards Yakima, Washington, home to red and green delicious apples and malicious black and white narcotics. I can tell you this, I didn't give a fig about fruit. My junkie color wheel was stuck in a gray area. This was just before I signed up long-term as Federal inmate #07384-085 in Oregon, for a decade of shits and giggles.

Yakima has extreme seasons, so when I showed up in September it was scorching. And since I owned nothing, I was dressed for the weather but not success. I wore flip-flops, cargo shorts with lots of pockets to fill, a tank top and a baseball cap. It wouldn't have been so hard to pick me out of a line up. In Seattle, when in the throes and short on mad money, I'd pop into a fiend-friendly Safeway or some other bloated carrier of America's prime cut artery hardeners for relief. I'd load up, then have a blowout sale at the nearest dive bar, where, for the price of bologna, drunken meat eaters would sink their teeth into my cut rate deals. If I happened to get punched in the face, I'd have something to help with the swelling.

Yakima's problem children swarmed the aisles like bees in a French boulangerie, especially after sunset. Competition for all things not nailed down was fierce. Store security had me pinned for a malignant meathead and weren't having any of it. I'd gotten a little lost in my invincibility while pretending to be citizen shopper. I was tackled and body slammed just outside the door.

There was no meat on my bones, but plenty I'd just stolen in my cargo shorts. The heroin I'd taken prior did a decent job of lessening the pain of my tenderized shoulder.

Bewildered, I got stuffed back in the can. To recalibrate my moral compass, I read books to an illiterate for seventy-five days, then got out and very quickly got lost again. The weather hadn't prepared for my release. Thanksgiving of '92 was twenty degrees with a foot of snow on the ground. I must have been quite the sight wandering the streets at night while half naked. With no coat and no heroin to lessen the sting, my pain was real.

I'm a survivor, so I sucked it up and did what I had to do. I marched over to the Union Gospel Mission like I was the chosen one. I feigned belief and swapped out my summertime junkie's uniform for an oversized sterilized set of hand me downs. I weighed about one hundred thirty-five pounds at the time. After a sing along, I had a shower and a hot meal. I parked my bedroll and settled into the smell of crack vapors off gassing through the poor's pores. I knew there were people out there able to hold it together, but believed that, alone and discarded, I was destined to ride my discomfort to a potter's field. The way I'd been operating, thirty-two felt like the outer limits of life on Earth. As a drug-fueled nihilist, I thought, *Who cares?*

For two and a half months, I mourned the loss of what propped me up. My predicament qualified me for a State sponsored halfway house. Enter Wayne—Lord of the manor. Wayne trolled the county jail and Union Gospel Mission for down and out men he could "rescue." Lonely and hungry, I was called to court. He interviewed me from up high on his Lazy-Boy and deemed me sufficiently pathetic. That qualified me for public assistance. I had mixed feelings: go inside where it was warm or limp towards another felony on my chemical crutches.

Wayne marched me down to the Department of Social and Health Services and got his man on the inside to set me up on the gravy train. I was allotted $335 a month, plus food stamps. After Wayne laid out the particulars of my financial obligations, I gleaned that I was just another disposable block of dole crammed into that single family dwelling that made up the foundation of his pyramid scheme. He carved out a two by six-foot space for me alongside the myriad thirty other male indigents on the floor. I was slightly cheesed off.

Wayne, a dead ringer for Kenny Rogers, had set up a nifty racket for himself. He didn't *own* the house full of broken hostages who signed over their dignity and government stipends. He sublet. His rent was cheap and his risk was minimal, but his instincts were animal. If it all went south, he could just pack a bag and skedaddle. No fuss, no muss. I must admit it was such a shrewd dope fiend move, I was a little envious.

Wayne planned to expand his empire by opening school of grift satellite campuses. He wanted to set up additional dole recipients in other rental houses. His top suck-ups would play pimp until they all went to jail or the government went broke. There's no shortage of indigents in Yakima. As a narcotics hub, the street crawled with qualified prospects.

Everyone at Wayne's World worked at his pleasure. I was a cook/scullery maid. One poor schmuck did Wayne's washing and ironing because, according to Wayne, "You gotta know when to fold 'em," and if there was any back talk, "know when to scold 'em."

As a stark raving sober alcoholic lost in his proclivities, Wayne rode a villainous pink cloud. The household shopping took place at Discount Co-op, where everything was dirt cheap. Wayne did his own shopping uptown. Residents were forced to smoke generics while Wayne smoked Camels. Can you imagine? My lungs burned with resentment.

Wayne's protégé, Barney—I knew his name was Barney because it was sewn onto his coveralls—oversaw hand-picking a crack team. Twelve skinny have-nots piled into Wayne's 1975 Cadillac Fleetwood nine passenger sedan. It was a hundred forty-four-mile ride across the mountains back to civilization. The goal was to cut through the grease of Seattle's Saturday car auctions and gather up as many clunkers as there were bodies to drive them. A caravan ensued. The neighbors weren't so thrilled with the new lawn ornaments.

Besides busted knuckles and an attaboy, who knows what unconscionable bennies Barney the mechanic reaped for wrenching on jalopies in the freezing cold. He was dedicated, seeing as how his leg was in a cast. Wayne bankrolled the buying frenzy courtesy of the constellation of burnouts he'd squeeze who camped on his floor and the dependably blue politicians of Washington State. The gas-guzzling American behemoths Wayne selected limped back, to be fixed up and rolled onto a used car lot where Billy worked. Billy was one of Wayne's hardened faves and former cellmate of James Fogle of *Drugstore Cowboy* fame. A plethora of Yakima's drug dealers pored over the stock on that lot, to rotate their fleet and stay under the police radar. It was all in the family at Wayne's World.

This brief episode was the appetizer before my six-month binge at the bank robbery buffet, ensuing incarceration and my new appreciation for a less frenetic life that continues to delight and never disappoints.

Chapter 29

Paris Emptied Out and Then Some

There was a brief window during the pandemic when the government let some of the choice museums receive a limited number of guests. Word barely got out before the window closed.

Terrell's solo show was scheduled to open the week France shut down for Covid.

I was lucky to happen upon the good news. To stand alone in a room lit up by the colors of Van Gogh's masterworks in the Musée d'Orsay was electrifying. I've been in chez Vince when I could barely get a glimpse beyond the selfie stick contingency who peddle their self-proclaimed auras of awesomeness. Yet there I was, alone with Van Gogh for fifteen minutes experiencing the kind of intimacy enjoyed by a nighttime security guard. I had to fight the urge to take a selfie of my own and just let the experience stand on its own instead.

My wife and I were two of the scant few art-deprived patrons in the former train station turned museum. The d'Orsay is a massive space with the world's largest collection of Impressionists, Post-Impressionists and Pointillists. Prior to the pandemic, the thought of riding a bicycle on the empty streets of Paris to visit an empty museum would have seemed fantastical.

The Arc de Triomphe, the Eiffel Tower, the Golden Arches? Some businesses shuttered along Rue de Rivoli during Covid, which blighted Paris with a different kind of virus, multi-nationals with an embarrassment of riches. That's not to say the government didn't make business owner's exits survivable, they did. France spent 240 billion euros to keep the economy afloat. My friend's restaurant was on a street that had a major gas explosion pre-Covid. The whole block was shut down for close to six months. When he did get back up and running, he decided to sell, had a buyer and was ready to pen the deal. Then Covid hit. The government stepped in to pay him and his employees. But if a restaurant closed on a tourist heavy street, you can bet your lunch money McDonald's would be there to insert their greasy meat hooks, which they did twice on Rue du Rivoli during Covid. I'm not lovin' it.

Shortly after the initial, *Oh god, we're all going to die,* phase of Covid, I entered the revived website of Doctolib—France's socialized medicine portal— and was able to step over enough bodies of the deniers to track down the sole remaining dose of the coveted Pfizer vaccine.

I made an appointment to get my inaugural jab. I was astonished to suddenly find myself in the sixty to sixty-nine-year-old category, which put me closer to dying and staying alive at the same time.

The mass jabbing was to take place at *Stade de France*, the stadium in Saint-Denis just north of Paris, where a portion of the 2015 terrorist attack took place during a soccer game. And more recently, the site for the closing ceremonies of the Paris Olympics. Although my wife was still in the 55 to 59 age group and according to Doctolib's website not yet eligible for the vacine, she held my hand and offered to translate.

We snaked our way to the front of the line, where she explained to the weaponless security guards that her stunted husband didn't speak much French. The two strapping Frenchmen sung a duet, "Non." Then they reconsidered their station and said, "Better go ask her," pointing to a woman of a certain age and stature who, if not the head of French society, was certainly the neck. My story is littered with examples of strong women who paved the way for me to thrive. I put my wife at the top of that list.

Terrell made her pitch on my behalf. "Madame, bonjour." Genuflect. "I am here to assist my husband with the language."

Madame said, "I will assess his level of comprehension. Say something in French."

I answered, "Oui?"

She responded to Terrell, "Yes, you had better go with him. And you should get *your* shot as well. Tell them Delphine sent you."

Dropping the name Delphine stood down security and carved a path forward. I was able to present my medical card and residence permit for access. Gifts I received from other French women who grease the gears of bureaucracy. The firemen on site were responsible for administering the jabs. The lines were long but *pompiers* are so revered, many would've doubled up just to get another look at the handsome lads. This difficult time made it clear to me that French socialism really does serve the needs of the people.

Prior to Terrell's third visa renewal she received an email from the immigration office that gave us both pause. It was encrypted, so we didn't fully understand. Three people we know recommended the same French immigration attorney, so we called him with a question. He agreed to take us for an emergency meeting on the upcoming Saturday in preparation for our Monday morning turn in the barrel. The single question of, *Why did they cancel my artist's visa?* morphed into a three-hour session.

There was a misunderstanding with my wife's visa. She got an additional design designation from the Chamber of Commerce, which allowed her to float down another income stream. As it turns out, this was a big no-no. She had *la crème de la crème* artist visa, which is held in high regard, but as any artist can tell you, making art and selling art are two different animals. She inadvertently opted to tag on as a lowly artisan so she could make a living. When it comes to work designations, France comes from the, *Stay in your own lane* and *no second helpings* point of view.

She said to the lawyer, "I made a mistake getting a second designation, didn't I?" He said, "It was more than a mistake, it was a betrayal. France gave you the highest designation and you traded down." He said they considered it a slap in the face. That time, my wife did cry. And cried and cried. I let him squirm while, stone faced, I bored holes in him with my ex-con laser beam eyes, but still had to pay for his time. I wanted to get my 500 € worth. I took note of the row of unopened Heinekens on his shelf that he'd be knocking back just as soon as we left. I pulled up a vision from yesteryear, my international collection of empty beer bottles. Almost art. At the time, as close to world travel as I got. Unfortunately, with the pickled mind of a sober alcoholic, I can never again think like a cucumber.

Artists are considered the top of the pecking order, an order of significance established by Colbert, King Louis XIV's Comptroller-General of Finances. The Heineken drinking lawyer told me that I'd have to get my own designation—which I'd already done—because, as a hitchhiker on Terrell's visa, I'd officially been kicked out of the car. "Plus," he said to me, "you're not making enough money." I thought, *No shit Sherlock*.

What he did provide that has been very helpful was a color-coded template of what paperwork the visa office requires and in what order. Information we hadn't found anywhere else.

Civil Status:

Convocation (directive to show up)

Feuille de renseignements (cover letter, optional)

Passporte (passport)

La carte de séjour (residency card)

Bail (rental agreement)

EDF facture (electric bill)

L'acte de naissance (birth certificate)

12-18 mois de relevés bancaires (bank statements)

Urssaf (social charges)

Paiements trimestrielle (quarterly payments)

Certificate of Vigilance (proof of no debt to government)

Impôts (the French tax authority)

Declarations des revenues (multiple years earnings report)

Avis d'Impositon, (tax return)

Attestation de couverture (proof of health insurance)

This secret info paid dividends in the expediency of subsequent visa appointments. The gatekeepers get frustrated with foreigners fumbling around for the right paperwork, often ending the appointment and essentially telling the freaked out aspiring citizen, *We're done here, you can make another appointment when you have your shit together. Bye now and have a nice day.* Because there are no partitions while on the cattle call, I've seen plenty of it.

Stopping traffic so the taxi van can deliver Terrell's art for her solo show. Rachida Dati, France's Minister of Culture, invited Terrell to show there. Not a bad endorsement.

The good news is, Terrell can still make and sell art. The lack of a talent visa just means she'll have to go through the artisan visa process more regularly until she gets citizenship, which is just around the corner.

The expat community I've lumped myself in with seemed a bit frigid when I arrived. I shower, I shave, I use deodorant. My manners are passable and my fly is generally zipped. Why the cold snub? When someone like me says, "Here I am. I'm making a go of it and am here to stay." They think, *Yeah, right, we've heard that one before.* After investing some of their finite energy, they're a bit standoffish, opting to view the proceedings from afar. Non-committed and inching closer only after some time goes by. Let's face it, sometimes energy is best left in the tank, because many of us who attempt the move are in the last chapter, shuffling towards Depends. I liken the situation to the Hitchcock movie, *Lifeboat*, where the expat population gradually decreases as conflict ensues. I'm still in the middle of the boat, where others have stubbed a toe, or fallen overboard and been eaten by the French bureaucracy sharks. After all I've been through, my French friends now consider me a Parisian. So—in full, self-protection mode—I too can pick and choose which bright-eyed, stargazing expats are serious about making the move and in need of my assistance.

I've been in Paris long enough that I'm starting to get invited to some of the marathon meals the French are famous for. I'm more of a barnyard Molière than a café club Voltaire. My education is of a different variety and I can only speak on what I know. So, when the crowd started to out-philosophize each other, I went low.

I was at a dinner put on by someone who'd previously hosted dinners for foreign dignitaries at the World Economic Forum in Davos. Man had he hit the skids inviting the likes of me. Not only was I a decade older than the next oldest person at the table, I was the only one there ever to don a blue collar. I'd entered through the service door.

I was listening to one of the international AI gods from Google wax poetic about its development. "As far as humans are concerned," he said, "one day we won't even be able to tell the difference." A clear indication he wasn't getting any. He interspersed that uncomfortable thought with a dissertation on the positive properties of microdosing LSD. I thought, *Yeah, that's the guy we need running the show.* I sized up the others around the table and wondered who would be willing to help me tie him up and park him in a closet until the AI thing blew over.

He claimed to be from Seattle, one of the upper echelon tech transplants responsible for carving out the soul of the city. I was not in agreement so I gave him a sneer and conceded that if he was right about AI, he'd soon be let go by monsters of his own making before the Cyborgs turned to march on humanity.

I seized the moment to turn myself into a zoo animal by introducing myself as an ex-junkie bank robber, which stole the remainder of his thunder. Suddenly, I was more interesting than AI and all eyes were on me. I threw in, "I'm a *lifelong* Seattleite," so as not to be confused with any recently installed brogrammers. I thought about the fleet of Google cars in Seattle affixed with telescoping cameras. "I will listen to you intently but will never spy on you or sell your information." It was the second such dinner I'd had with that crowd. There would be no third.

OLYMPIC SECURITY PEOPLE WERE NICE

I'm usually not one to initiate conversations with the police. Historically, it's always been the other way around. Even though in my early life I was anything but law abiding, I've never not considered their value. Even at one hundred thirty pounds, whacked-out and with the hungry look of a feral animal, I often felt comforted by their presence. A ticket to get out of the rain. A ride to rehab. An orange onesie. Glass half full.

As the 2024 Summer Olympics approached, France geared up for nefarious elements bent on spoiling the party. The police presence was beyond massive. Bloated police vans snaked around every point of interest, blaring sirens just to be heard.

On day one, there was an act of sabotage on the railway systems of three major cities that lead into Paris, just hours before the opening ceremonies. I was in the Musée du Carnavalet, admiring a painting of Paris burning, when I heard about the attack. Blame laid, not on the usual suspects, but pinned on the French far left and environmental activists. Disruption was the point. I aimed to thank the groups of *gendarmes* I saw milling about. There was no threat from itchy Taser fingers, no "Keep moving, asshole," and no icy stares. Instead, every one of them thanked me for thanking them, for which I said, *"Je vous en prie."*

Chapter 30

Fifty Shades of Gravy

Over the course of my post-prison culinary adventure, I transmogrified from bottom feeder into a free-range West Coast foodie snob. No more industrial chickens, gas station corn dogs, Velveeta or bleached bread for me. Once I pivoted away from prison Nutraloaf, and into a position where I could make my own choices, I started to subscribe to the notion of garbage in, garbage out.

Pre-virus, before the temporary death of all the restaurants, and before all the young cyber slackers were forced to learn how to cook, Seattle was a pretty good place to shoot a wad on global cuisine. Tom Douglas was always happy to eat your paycheck. And there was a time when Puget Sound seafood couldn't be beat. Then salmon started testing positive for meth, Oxy and Viagra. What kind of school are *they* attending?

After watching a horrifying documentary on America's sleazy mega meat producers, titled *Vegucated,* my wife and I had a good long cry and pitched our tent in camp vegan. The tears lasted two years, until we landed in France. A native quickly noted, "You don't drink, you don't smoke, you don't eat meat or cheese, what are you doing in France?" I thought, *Well, they do take care of their animals here, until it's off with their heads.* Permission to backslide granted. Vegans with benefits. I used to be a wedgetarian, I only ate slices of pizza or cake.

Before moving, I concluded that the mecca of food snobbery *had* to be Paris. This, from an outsider with opinions yet fully formed. I saw the rosy glow on Parisian faces as they walked down the street. Not the smug look of a braggart, or the veined rosacea of a topped off wino, but the organic look of good health. The only look they'd ever known. Over here, consumers benefit from the high standards set in place by their government and the farmers who produce the food.

In prison, with elbows out and head down scanning the crowd for stabbings, I used to fist my plastic spork and pack my jowls to capacity with food stuff—liver and onions, Noodles Jefferson, the aforementioned Nutraloaf, etc.—for expediency. The threat of lockdown and brown bag baloney sandwiches was a constant. It was a race against the clock, to make room for the next batch of sad sacks in a rush to nowhere. Then came the hurried exodus from the chow hall, on to the next event that would keep the clock moving closer to my release date. I was lucky enough to have a release date. If it can be helped, never eat anywhere called Chow Hall.

By comparison, meals in France are more laid-back, often multi-course, two-hour affairs. With a scant, thirty-five-hour work week and early retirement etched into their psyche, there's plenty of time for the French to loll about in café restaurants. As a free man, I too prefer the slow tick of the clock over the frenetic pace in the U.S.

The bar is high. Check any lunch menu from a French grade school and you won't find weenies trembling under a blanket. You will find racks of lamb with oven roasted potatoes called *la Bonnette*, grown in sand on Noirmoutier island—it's the iodine in the kelp that sets them apart—massaged in olive oil with a rosemary garnish, asparagus and *crème brûlée* for dessert. I took language classes at Alliance Francaise, just so I could fine dine in the cafeteria for six euros. I still struggle with the language, but I *do* know how to eat.

With over 44,000 restaurants in Paris to choose from, the choice is not always clear. I crave good Mexican food. Pre-Covid I discovered a decent joint in the 19th arrondissement and commenced to wear it out. My heart broke watching the French eat tacos with a knife and fork and without hot sauce. Most French don't brave the heat—an insufferable affront to my senses. I was forced to model barbarism by loading up with the unemployed tomatillo sauce, leaning into my tacos sideways and shoving them into my bottomless pie hole. Park the flat wear compadre. Message received. I made savages out of the lot of them.

Come to find out, many so called restaurants in Paris don't cook. And you wouldn't know from their prices that they microwave frozen blocks of food stuff. They call it *ready to serve*—freezer to table in five minutes. When it comes to Steak tartar with a raw egg on top—that cat food doppelganger—there's not even a *need* for a microwave. Terrell saw a pallet of single serving steak tartar wrapped in plastic sitting in the sun in front of a restaurant. I don't know who thought that was a good idea, but I'll bet the chef's name is *Hurl*, and not with a silent H.

Righteous home cookin' joints found themselves forced to lower prices to compete. It's become such a stain on the French tablecloth and cultural heritage status, that the Minister of Trade floated a transparency bill in Parliament, as an attempt to level the playing field.

My favorite place for takeout is *Avec Ceux Ci*, a five-star joint just a few blocks from my apartment. It's impossible to walk by without my nose diverting me to drop some serious coin. It's run by Big Chef and Little Chef and has become a weekly guilty pleasure for the four plus years I've been in the neighborhood. I choose an item and they say, "*Avec ceux-ci?*" (What would you like to go with that?) I point and grunt, "Ça." Again, they prod me and on it goes until my bag is heavy and my wallet light. I cross the freebie line at about fifty euros and get tossed a couple of dense mini loaves of bread packed with funky fromage.

Word got out that Terrell and I were preparing a Christmas time meal and we were gifted a petite, but very expensive slab of foie gras with a mondo chunk of truffle inside. To me, truffle has always smelled like someone else's dirty gym socks. A thoughtful gift but—double retch—I'd rather have gotten a box of Cracker Jacks. Foie gras is the black-hearted bi-product of force-feeding mammoth ducks to enlarge their livers. Medically it's referred to as hepatic steatosis, which for me—as a former owner of an enlarged liver, due to hepatitis C—no matter the species, is a condition to avoid. Especially at the dinner table.

He asked if I liked foie gras. I told him I'd never tried it, even though I did try it at a French dinner party and had a serious a gag reflex that I didn't want to involuntarily pull back up. Terrell had the same reaction. He said, "Just put it on a piece of toast as an appetizer." I just nodded and said, "Ah!" *What did he say, just put it in the toilet and flush?* When we got home, we just couldn't, so down the waste pipe it went. I'm sorry for the duck, but eating its diabolically tampered with liver isn't a sign of respect and it sure isn't going to bring it back. *C'est la vie, c'est la mort.*

When we got here, Terrell asked an elderly French woman, "*Excusez moi Madame, où est la* canned pumpkin?" We got no verbal response, only a finger wagged like a metronome, much too close to Terrell's face. She then pointed to the produce section. Tough loved into buying a fresh pumpkin, we've never looked back.

I've discovered my new favorite joint, right on my street. GEMÜSE - Berliner Kebap serves shaved rotisserie chicken, roasted red bell peppers and zucchini with fresh purple cabbage and secret Algerian sauce stuffed in home-made pitas for 8,50 €. It's so popular, there's six people in that hole in the wall going gang busters six days a week. Ask a local, the best deals are always off the beaten path.

I also fancy La Grande Épicerie de Paris, 312,000 square feet of gastro-intestinal bliss. Like a modern-day crack dealer, they can count on my return week after week. I have a friend who says, "You can tell a person's values by looking in their check register. What's important to me? Food, food, food, food, food.

Thanksgiving is a holiday I've never been able to wrap my head around. My mom used to wrap mondo Butterball turkeys, with their unreliable pop-up turkey timers, in bacon sweaters before they went in the oven. The result was birds floating in their pans of grease, yet so dry they begged to be drowned in gravy for a second death.

All that preparation to get together with family, not talk to each other, dutifully mow through the offerings like locusts, then clean-up for an hour, snooze in a tryptophan stupor in front of a television stuck on a meaningless game of football, while trying to comprehend the true spirit of the holiday. Nonetheless, I can't seem to let it go.

Melancholy for the above creeps up on me as the curious day approaches. Possibly over the loss of those calorie packed, indelible episodes of silence. I have fond memories of the lonely, depressing event where alcohol, introverts and turkeys unite. So, putting on a big, hyped-up meal seems to be an adequate antidote for my seasonal blues. It's a good thing I love to cook.

Our first Thanksgiving in Paris, Terrell and I were tripping over each other in a three hundred-fifty square foot apartment with a Barbie sized kitchen. The only place to prep food was a cutting board we bought to place over the sink. Still, we pulled off the full complement. All the lonely Americans had already been kidnapped and were gorging on melancholy elsewhere, so we scrounged up a young, hungry Aussie as confused about the concept as I was. He was lonely and in love with a Parisian gal, who didn't love him back. Both lovely people who yo-yo in and out of town on occasion.

We absorbed his pain while stuffing him with spatchcock turkey—split down the backbone and flattened to remain moist and avoid being like a Blunderball—sheep's cheese mashed potatoes, brussels sprouts topped with *lardons* (bacon) and homemade pumpkin pie with a quinoa flour crust. No shortcuts and very labor intensive. It didn't patch up his broken heart, but it sure took care of his stomach and our need to feed.

SEATTLEITES SAVE MY BACON

An acquaintance of my wife from thirty years ago wondered what became of Terrell and looked her up on Instagram. This curious woman is a lawyer who, for many years worked for a major Seattle art gallery on intellectual property rights. She's also a francophile who speaks impeccable French.

She said to Terrell, "Is there anything I can do to help you? I have a lot of time on my hands." Terrell was just then reconstructing her website to include the required French legalese. She spent countless hours helping Terrell not only with her website but with her art career as well. And she ended up buying a two hundred fifty-year-old apartment which she hired Terrell and me to bring back to life.

After we finished the project, she and her husband had a soirée—to schmooze and show off their beautifully refurbished apartment. In attendance was a scrum of Americans she plucked off the street, pickle ball court, bibliothèque, etc. All the bold moves Americans must make to stave off loneliness in a foreign country. An architect who works at the American Embassy was in attendance. She had a rigid air about her and we both thought we'd somehow made it on her shit list, but when we were heading for the door, she snatched Terrell up for a big American hug. It just goes to show, what I think isn't always factual. She offered to get us into the Ambassador's residence for a tour, which we went on shortly thereafter.

There are many doors in Paris, inaccessible to the common person. The ones to the Ambassador's residence were at least twenty feet tall. The door opened and we showed our passports. The guard said, "Do you have a pass?"

We said, "No pass, just passports."

He said, "Wait here," took our passports and closed the door, leaving us in a snowstorm on the street. I hesitated to hand it over. It's not a great feeling when a stranger takes your passport and disappears. My reaction was, *We are sooo fucked.* Then the door opened, and we went inside.

We were a group of thirteen. The tour guide was an elderly French woman who was married to a diplomat and had worked at the American Embassy periodically over the years—a fountain of information. I fact checked. She knew her stuff.

The original property popped up in seventeen twenty and passed through a series of owners until 1836, when Baroness Pontalba purchased the property and hired Louis Visconti to design the house that would replace the existing one.

BACKSTORY ON THE BARONESS

As a two-year-old, the New Orleans born Baroness inherited her father's fortune. Her mother, a savvy businesswoman grew the pile considerably. At age sixteen the Baroness married her cousin, *Yuck-o* and moved to France where she envisioned a swanky life in Paris. *Au contraire*. Instead, she was virtually imprisoned in a chateau in Bumfuck for twenty years. During that time, her father-in-law tried to wheedle her fortune, then ended up shooting her with a musket pistol at point blank range, four times. He knocked off one of her breasts and two fingers—but not the middle finger.

He was a terrible shot, until with the last ball of lead, shot himself dead. This allowed her to make her way to Paris and start work on her *hôtel particulier* or grand mansion. After her death, the property eventually found its way into the hands of the Rothschild family, who in 1938 fled to Switzerland. The property was then taken over by the Luftwaffe. After the war it went back to France. In 1948 it was sold to the U.S. government on the cheap and would eventually become the official residence of the American Ambassador.

As is the tradition, the Ambassador in service picks their own art. I was allowed to snap photos, including photos of photos, such as the Obama family, the Biden family—not 45 or his spawn—Oprah, Tony Bennett and Lady Gaga, to name a few, and to not name one. There was a little seen painting by Kehinde Wiley on loan, until he delivers the one commissioned. A gorgeous portrait of singer, dancer and freedom fighter Josephine Baker, whose memory will live in the Panthéon (she's actually buried in Monaco) and in the hearts of the French for all eternity. A painting of George Washington, sitting on his literal high horse is at the top of a sweeping staircase. We met the staff preparing Thanksgiving dinner a week early for the French. They broke out the ancient Limoges dinner ware for the occasion. Then there was all the millwork, furniture, etc. For a guy without a pass and no credentials, I felt a keen sense of belonging.

NOVEMBER 6, 2024, MESSAGE VALIDATED. *VIVE LA FRANCE!*

It's November 25, 2024. As I write this, I'm on the third month of a media blackout. I can't escape a trickle of information, but for now, I'm not seeking it out. The firehose will hit me after January 20. For sanity's sake, semi-ignorance is bliss—but only if I stay true to the exercise. After crawling out of my end-of-times bunker, I rolled up my sleeves and surprisingly serene, decided to go to work—work that feeds my soul.

I remember a conversation I had with someone who took the same stance eight years ago and I thought, *How can you not want to know what's going on? We need to do something.* Now I *am* doing something. It's six a.m. and I'm writing this. Doomscrolling is a zero-sum game—a steady stream of negative displaces all that is good. So, out of sight, out of mind. I'm taking care of my mental health.

I have a mentor who, during the '09 housing market crash, when I was severely depressed and about to lose my house, told me, "*When you wake up, get up.*" That simple suggestion changed my life. Somehow, the sun still rose, and the coffee was on. I pulled through to remain upright and functional. When I open my eyes, I remember that phrase.

My screen time is down and my brain and blood pressure have stabilized and are resting. Plus, I'm writing. The best thing I can do is live each day as it unfolds and not fold in on myself. The elements I shut out would like nothing more than the whole world to be a trembling mass of despair.

Life is short and time waits for no one. It isn't something that I should be waiting for after x, y or z happens. I've squandered so much time only to remain outraged, it's time to save what's left for myself. I want to spend my time on things that bring me joy. Feeding the lunatic fringe is no longer where I'll park my lunch money. I don't want to be perpetually punched in the face by people who like to break things. I'll pick and choose my battles to live a good life full of love, humor, friendship and creativity. Economies are personal. The business of life will be my safe harbor while the hot spots burn around me. This will be my antidote to counter all the haters. I choose to thrive and not give oxygen to a fire that tries to consume me. I invite you to come and join me.

DECEMBER 11, 2024

Terrell had her naturalization interview yesterday at the *préfecture de Paris* on rue Ursins, Île Saint-Louis. I helped her study for a month for something she'd been preparing for all her life. Because of the emotional overwhelm, the documents requested by the *préfecture's* website seemed like hundreds but were only about forty, going back two generations. Still, a monumental task which involved hustling the Alabama and Texas vital records departments and then having everything translated into French by a court certified translator. Many were time sensitive and some had to be requested a second time because of expiration dates. All the documents were to be uploaded onto their site, but Terrell showed up with printed copies too, just in case.

A friend who recently went through the process said, "Don't take anything personally. There's no rhyme or reason to the process. Think of it as an endurance test." Terrell didn't flinch, she showed up with extras. The young woman interviewing her asked for only two.

We printed seven single spaced pages of questions from the *préfecture's* site that were said to be part of the quiz. Laws, dates, births, deaths, kings, queens, artists, the function of the government, monuments, definitions of laws, Congress' role, the Senate's role, philosophers, wars, generals, singers, food, and on and on. Terrell was asked very little.

She was told, "It will take five to eight months, unless it takes a year," to know the verdict.

Terrell said, "That's a long time to wonder." Parting words were given. "Live your life," the young woman said.

Terrell struck up a conversation with the security guard on her way out. The day before was the opening of Notre Dame—which is just a couple blocks away and the security guard was there on his detail. He said, "Trump is big, he takes up a lot of space."

Terrell thought, *No kidding*. "He's very sick," she said.

The guard said, "It's because of all of his power, isn't it?"

"Unfortunately," she said.

Chapter 31
Post Script Wrap-up

Why should chronic sufferers of francophilia take notice of my trajectory? Like Terrell's Texas grandmother used to say, "If it's true, it ain't braggin." I wake up every day on fire with gratitude that we were able to experience such an epic move. A work assignment with relocation package didn't send us. Deep pockets didn't pave our way. We didn't pack our bags on a whim and no one forced us out. We didn't know anyone, nor get to jump the queue when we got here. With so many things out of my control, I still can't pinpoint the exact how of it. Blind faith definitely played its part.

On some days, the best I can be is a liquified container of uncertainty leaking a trail of self-doubt. But a little imposter syndrome never stopped me. I stay on the conveyor belt a day at a time and act as if, with the notion that each day will take care of itself. So long as I stay in my lane and keep my past in the past. I approached the move to France with both eyes open, willing to take risks and willing to fail while trying not to swallow my adam's apple.

Really, all I did to get here was follow my wife and eventually my own heart. I've asked loads of questions, filled out reams of paperwork—*one sheet at a time*—and put one foot in front of the other. I brought my solid American work ethic with me and it has paid dividends. Even at my lowest, I've never been lazy. It takes extreme diligence to support a $500 a day habit without a job. Action, action, action has always been my recipe. I'm also a bit of a dreamer slash hallucinator and that doesn't hurt either. Half-baked is halfway there.

I chose to intersperse a good chunk of my old life in the story to show how unlikely it is for a guy like me to have landed on my feet in Paris. Possible but not probable, it's just what happened. Once sober, my all-incompassing negativity no longer consumed me. The will to live took over the space where my drugged-fueled nihilism had wreaked havoc. This cosmic shift allowed me to think for myself. The many facets of the world started to come into focus and my experiences took on meaning. When the immigration process started twenty-four years later, I plowed ahead, because over the course of my sober life I've learned that little steps always add up to leaps and bounds. Even when I ran into hiccups while preparing, I kept marching purposefully towards my vision of Paris. I got out of my own way, and left the results up to my team of intangibles more suited to determine the outcome. I tell this story as an everyman invitation.

I've come to love France. It's essentially a big farm with a few cities plugged in here and there. Sometimes I forget that this is the capital. I walk by the *Assemblée nationale,* France's congressional building and think, *They're in there doing the work of the people.* I no longer think that about the U.S. There's an atmosphere of togetherness between the government and the general public that I never experienced in the States. I see it and feel it and I benefit from it. I'm sure some of that feeling of togetherness has to do with my close proximity to others. As the most densely populated city in Europe, Parisians seem to get along just fine without too much drama. If a woman—of any nationality—is in the metro with her baby in a stroller and trying to go up or down a set of stairs, people practically beat each other back to be the first to lend a hand. Having gone through a revolution and two world wars on their own soil, France has been through plenty, and hasn't forgotten what abject cruelty looks like. Or maybe that's just the way the French are wired.

Malheureusement, I still speak bastardized French, but to the delight of the natives, *"Excusez-moi, ma* [sic] *français et n'est pas très bon."* I make a solid effort every day and don't feel judged here for my inadequacies. I know my accent and language skills are subpar but—as hard as the language is for me—people are overjoyed that I continue to make an effort and kindly offer corrections when I'm in error. I appreciate that. Public education is top notch here. I've witnessed hundreds of teenagers crammed into public libraries plowing through their homework. A high school degree here in Paris approaches the level of a college degree in the States—even though high schoolers here get Wednesday afternoons off. I feel at ease living in a united Europe full of educated people. And my central nervous system is thankful.

Before we came to Paris, we envisioned what type of person we wanted to rent from—kind, generous, willing to help us gain a toehold. We made vision boards and stated our intention to the universe—a universe I've come to realize is inviting and self-organizing. I know, airy-fairy, but hey, we were willing to go anywhere for assistance. We discovered that with French bureaucracy, banking, etc., *non* is an automatic response and just around the corner from yes.

We continue to integrate. We reach out and ask for help from locals we've met along the way. The rest we do on the fly. My wife learned *La Marseillaise*, the French national anthem, as part of her studies for French citizenship. Based on my level of French, I'm a couple of years away, but closer than I was yesterday. And in all interactions, I never forget—*it's très important*—to lead with a supplication. It is their country and their tradition. I'm a guest here. A kind word or gesture goes a long way towards acclimation wherever you are. With what I've learned throughout my journey, I'm able and willing to help others who are keen on making the leap towards this invaluable experience.

According to how favorably my chips have landed, I believe there's been something nebulous in play that has helped move us along. In prison, intuition kept me out of a lot of scrapes. I've learned to listen to the whispers. When everything in the world is so loud, the whispers may have been what delivered me down the homestretch to France's welcome mat.

Vive la France !

Terrell on a horsehair upholstered bench at the Louvre with our friend Mike Reid, who visits during Fashion Week, in the distance.

Me at a community event in an 18th c. Hôtel particulier on rue Poitier.

Estrogen Rising, a novel, coming soon!   *Cover art by Terrell Lozada*

Acknowledgement

First and foremost, thanks to my wife Terrell, who has always believed in me, helped quell my freakouts and in addition to the cover art—line by line—stepped in to prop me up. She was monumental on this project. Also, thanks to my editor Fran Lebowitz, who encouraged me to lose the space exploration and come back down to Earth to write from my heart, she's a gem. And thanks to the city of Paris and all my newfound friends for providing me with a new perspective.

www.ingramcontent.com/pod-product-compliance
Lightning Source LLC
LaVergne TN
LVHW051517070426
835507LV00023B/3162